A Fruitful Sunday and Other Short Stories

Dans la même collection :

Agatha Christie
The Actress and Other Short Stories

Roald Dahl
Someone like you and Other Short Stories
The Hitch-Hiker and Other Short Stories

Graham Greene
The Third Man

Mary Higgins Clark
Terror Stalks the Class Reunion

James Joyce
Dubliners

Ruth Rendell
Walter's Leg and Other Short Stories

Collectifs
Thirteen Modern English and American Short Stories
English Ghost Stories
English Crime Stories of Today
The Umbrella Man and Other Short Stories (premières lectures)

ISBN : 978-2-253-08409-9 – 1re publication

Collection « Lire en anglais »
fondée par Henri Yvinec

Agatha Christie

A Fruitful Sunday and Other Short Stories

Présentation et annotations par Lise Bloch,
professeur agrégé

et Françoise Thomas-Garnier,
professeur certifié

avec la collaboration de C. M. Mayrhofer
M. A. (Cantab) Phd (ANU)

Le Livre de Poche

Abbreviations

adj	adjective
cf	confer (see)
cond	conditional
comp	comparative
fam	familiar
pl	plural *(pluriel)*
pp	past participle *(participe passé)*
pret	preterit
qch	*quelque chose*
qq	*quelqu'un*
sb	somebody
sg	singular *(singulier)*
sth	something
subj	subjunctive
sup	superlative
=	synonym
≠	antonym or different meaning from

Sommaire

La collection « Lire en anglais »

Tout naturellement, après quelques années d'étude d'une langue étrangère, naît l'envie de découvrir sa littérature. Mais le vocabulaire dont on dispose est souvent insuffisant ; la perspective de recherches lexicales multipliées chez le lecteur isolé, la présentation fastidieuse du vocabulaire, pour le professeur, sont autant d'obstacles redoutables. C'est pour tenter de les aplanir que nous proposons cette collection. Elle constitue une étape vers la lecture autonome, sans dictionnaire ni traduction, grâce à des notes facilement repérables.

Le lecteur trouvera :

En page de gauche

Des textes de grands auteurs choisis pour leur intérêt littéraire et la qualité de leur langue.

En page de droite

Des notes juxtalinéaires rédigées dans la langue du texte, qui aident le lecteur à :

Comprendre

Tous les mots et expressions difficiles contenus dans la ligne de gauche sont reproduits en caractères gras et expliqués dans le contexte ;

Observer

Des notes d'observation de la langue soulignent le caractère idiomatique de certaines tournures ou constructions ;

Apprendre

Dans un but d'enrichissement lexical, certaines notes proposent des synonymes, des antonymes, des expressions faisant appel aux mots qui figurent dans le texte.

C'est à dessein que quelques mots clés sont expliqués plus d'une fois. Ils sont alors présentés sous un autre angle, notamment à l'aide de nouveaux synonymes ou antonymes, plus adéquats dans un nouvel épisode de l'histoire. Ceci pourra également éviter des retours en arrière toujours fastidieux.

Vocabulaire en contexte

En fin de volume, une liste de mots contenus dans le texte, suivis de leur traduction, comporte les verbes irréguliers et les mots qui n'ont pas été annotés faute de place ou parce que leur sens était évident dans le contexte. Grâce à ce lexique, on pourra procéder à quelques vérifications ou faire un bilan des mots retenus au cours des lectures.

Henri Yvinec

Agatha Christie: A Profile

Agatha Christie (1890-1976) is definitely* not an author who needs to be introduced to readers of crime literature. Everybody knows of Hercule Poirot and of Miss Marple, and if we were asked where Miss Marple lives or what vegetable Poirot will grow* when he retires*, we would find the questions absurd.

Many of her stories are built like scenarios. This is particularly perceptible in the four psychological romance short-stories presented here. The minute* description of an evening dress, of a shying horse, of an old rattling car, the precise stage directions concerning movements, gestures, places, the signs of emotions which are noted, the cutting* clearly indicated, all of this makes the reader believe that he is at the theatre. In fact they are one-act plays divided into several scenes.

On the other hand, the scenery* is somewhat neglected, a drawing-room, a lane in the country or a tobacco shed are suggested in a few words, while the dialogues are long, repetitive, marking hesitation or silence, as it is in a normal conversation. The words, the turn of phrases which are used are ordinary and seem to have been recorded* without the characters'* knowledge. This is an element in Christie's writing that deserves* more recognition than it usually gets.

Moreover, especially in her short stories appears her belief that anybody can turn into a criminal, crook* or killer, as well as anybody can finish as a victim. Good and Evil perpetually fighting against each other. Happiness seldom* or never attained. She dares to allude to money matches*, suicide, and even prostitution in financial circles.

There, as it is well shown in these four short stories, Christie's fundamentals* are revealed, called moral rectitude, loyalty, fortitude*, fairness. But, at bottom, a basic optimism which she formulated herself: "Why should I give up any hope until one is dead?"

* cf Vocabulary, p. 108.

A Fruitful Sunday

'Well, really, I call this too delightful,' said Miss Dorothy Pratt for the fourth time. 'How I wish the old cat could see me now. She and her Janes!'

The 'old cat' thus scathingly alluded to was Miss Pratt's highly estimable employer, Mrs Mackenzie Jones, who had strong views upon the Christian names suitable for parlourmaids and had repudiated Dorothy in favour of Miss Pratt's despised second name of Jane.

Miss Pratt's companion did not reply at once – for the best of reasons. When you have just purchased a baby Austin, fourth hand, for the sum of twenty pounds, and are taking it out for the second time only, your whole attention is necessarily focused on the difficult task of using both hands and feet as the emergencies of the moment dictate.

'Er – ah!' said Mr Edward Palgrove, and negotiated a crisis with a horrible grinding sound that would have set a true motorist's teeth on edge.

'Well, you don't talk to a girl much,' complained Dorothy.

Mr Palgrove was saved from having to respond as at that moment he was roundly and soundly cursed by the driver of a motor omnibus.

'Well, of all the impudence,' said Miss Pratt, tossing her head.

'I only wish *he* had this foot brake,' said her swain bitterly.

'Is there anything wrong with it?'

'You can put your foot on it till kingdom comes,' said Mr Palgrove. 'But nothing happens.'

'Oh, well, Ted, you can't expect everything for twenty pounds. After all, here we are, in a real car, on Sunday afternoon going out of town the same as everybody else.'

More grinding and crashing sounds.

fruitful: signifies producing much fruit and, at the same time, producing good results

really: in fact • **call:** consider • **too delightful:** very pleasant
how I wish: I desire with force • **old cat:** disagreeable woman • **now:** at present • **her Janes:** her manner of giving me the name of "Jane"
thus: in this manner • **scathingly alluded to:** cited with sarcasm
highly: to a great degree
strong views: solid opinions • **suitable:** acceptable • **parlour-maids:** domestics • **repudiated Dorothy:** rejected the name of Dorothy • **despised:** detested
reply: answer • **at once:** immediately • **best of reasons:** very serious reason • **just purchased:** acquired recently • **baby Austin:** small car • **fourth hand:** you are proprietor number 4
only: just • **whole:** entire
focused: totally directed • **task:** job • **both:** the two
as: at the time that • **emergencies:** dangerous situations
negotiated a crisis: confronted a difficulty with success
grinding: very unpleasant • **set a ... on edge:** irritated a good car driver, made his teeth hypersensitive
a girl: Dorothy herself • **complained:** said in a plaintive voice

was saved ... respond: made his answer unnecessary • **as:** because • **roundly and soundly:** with brutality • **cursed:** covered with all the names imaginable • **motor omnibus:** bus
of all the impudence: extreme insolence • **tossing her head:** moving her head up in disapproval
foot brake: system for stopping the car • **swain:** boyfriend
bitterly: with a tone of reproach
anything wrong with it: a problem with the brake (note *with*)
till kingdom comes: waiting for the moment when the reign of God is established = a very long time • **nothing happens:** with no result
you can't expect: it is not reasonable of you to demand
after all: in conclusion • **on Sunday:** note *on*
going out: having an excursion • **the same ... else:** like the other persons • **crashing sounds:** violent bangs

'Ah,' said Ted, flushed with triumph. 'That was a better change.'

'You do drive something beautiful,' said Dorothy admiringly.

Emboldened by feminine appreciation, Mr Palgrove attempted a dash across Hammersmith Broadway, and was severely spoken to by a policeman.

'Well, I never,' said Dorothy as they proceeded towards Hammersmith Bridge in a chastened fashion. 'I don't know what the police are coming to. You'd think they'd be a bit more civil-spoken, seeing the way they've been shown up lately.'

'Anyway, I didn't want to go along this road,' said Edward sadly. 'I wanted to go down the Great West Road and do a bust.'

'And be caught in a trap as likely as not,' said Dorothy. 'That's what happened to the master the other day. Five pounds and costs.'

'The police aren't so dusty after all,' said Edward generously. 'They pitch into the rich, all right. No favour. It makes me mad to think of these swells who can walk into a place and buy a couple of Rolls-Royces without turning a hair. There's no sense in it. I'm as good as they are.'

'And the jewellery,' said Dorothy, sighing. 'Those shops in Bond Street. Diamonds and pearls and I don't know what! And me with a string of Woolworth pearls.'

She brooded sadly upon the subject. Edward was able once more to give full attention to his driving. They managed to get through Richmond without mishap. The altercation with the policeman had shaken Edward's nerve. He now took the line of least resistance, following blindly behind any car in front whenever a choice of thoroughfares presented itself.

In this way he presently found himself following a shady country lane which many an experienced motorist would have given his soul to find.

'Rather clever turning off the way I did,' said Edward, taking all the credit to himself.

flushed: red in the face (note *with* not *of*)
change: change of gear; gear box = *boîte de vitesses*
you do drive: you really operate the car • **something beautiful:** (a familiar expression) admirably well
emboldened: encouraged
attempted a dash across: tried to cut rapidly • **broadway:** large road • **spoken to:** reprimanded
well, I never: expresses indignation • **proceeded towards:** moved in the direction of • **chastened fashion:** disciplined manner
police are: note the plural • **coming to:** doing • **a bit:** a little
civil-spoken: polite • **way:** manner • **shown up:** revealed to be incompetent • **lately:** recently
anyway: in any case
sadly: with regret
do a bust: do a sprint, go very rapidly
caught...trap: arrested by surprise • **as likely as not:** probably
what happened: what was experienced • **the master:** my employer • **five pounds and costs:** penalty and a complementary tax
not so dusty: acceptably good (familiar expression)
pitch into: attack
makes me mad: irritates me considerably • **swells:** rich and snobbish persons • **walk into a place:** present themselves • **couple:** pair
without ... hair: insolently calm • **there's no sense in it:** it is contrary to logic • **good:** estimable • **jewellery:** precious personal ornaments • **sighing:** with regret • **Bond Street:** select street in London • **I don't know what:** all the rest of it • **string:** ornament around the neck • **Woolworth:** a popular chain of shops • **brooded:** meditated • **once more:** one more time • **driving:** manner of directing the car • **managed:** were able to • **get through:** traverse • **mishap:** incident • **shaken...nerve:** caused to tremble • **took the line...resistance:** chose the easy solution • **following... behind:** going immediately after without looking • **whenever:** every time • **thoroughfares:** roads for public traffic • **presently:** before long • **shady** ≠ in the sun • **country lane:** rural way • **many** a(n) + sg: a great number of (+ pl) • **soul:** most precious treasure
rather clever: very intelligent • **turning off:** taking another route
taking all ... to himself: as on his personal initiative

'Sweetly pretty, I call it,' said Miss Pratt. 'And I do declare, there's a man with fruit to sell.'

Sure enough, at a convenient corner was a small wicker table with baskets of fruit on it, and the legend EAT MORE FRUIT displayed on a banner.

'How much?' said Edward apprehensively, when frenzied pulling of the hand brake had produced the desired result.

'Lovely strawberries,' said the man in charge.

He was an unprepossessing-looking individual with a leer.

'Just the thing for the lady. Ripe fruit, fresh-picked. Cherries, too. Genuine English. Have a basket of cheeries, lady?'

'They do look nice ones,' said Dorothy.

'Lovely, that's what they are,' said the man hoarsely. 'Bring you luck, lady, that basket will.' He at last condescended to reply to Edward. 'Two shillings, sir, and dirt-cheap. You'd say so if you knew what was inside the basket.'

'They look awfully nice,' said Dorothy.

Edward sighed and paid over two shillings. His mind was obsessed by calculation. Tea later, petrol – this Sunday motoring business wasn't what you'd call *cheap*. That was the worst of taking girls out! They always wanted everything they saw.

'Thank you, sir,' said the unprepossessing-looking one. 'You've got more than your money's worth in that basket of cherries.'

Edward shoved his foot savagely down and the Baby Austin leaped at the cherry vendor after the manner of an infuriated Alsatian.

'Sorry,' said Edward. 'I forgot she was in gear.'

'You ought to be careful, dear,' said Dorothy. 'You might have hurt him.'

Edward did not reply. Another half-mile brought them to an ideal spot by the banks of a stream. The Austin was left by the side of the road and Edward and Dorothy sat affectionately upon the river bank and munched cherries. A Sunday paper lay unheeded at their feet.

sweetly pretty: perfect • **do declare:** emphasis of surprise
fruit: note the singular • **sell:** give in exchange for money
convenient: strategic • **wicker:** *osier*
eat: consume
displayed: arranged for public view
frenzied pulling: frenetic efforts to move
hand brake: system for stopping a car by hand.
strawberries: *fraises* • **man in charge:** vendor
unprepossessing: unpleasant • **leer:** repulsive look in the eyes
ripe: mature • **fresh-picked:** just taken from the plant
cherries: *cerises* • **genuine:** real

do look: give the impression of being
lovely: succulent • **hoarsely:** in a disagreeable voice
luck: good chance, prosperity
dirt-cheap: at an extremely low price
if you knew...: the phrase is very important for the story
awfully: very terribly
sighed: made the sound of respiration • **mind:** conscience
tea: to offer a cup of tea • **later:** some time after
motoring business: excursion with the car
worst: sup of *bad* • **taking ... out:** inviting for a tour
saw: remarked
one: man
your money's worth: the value of your money

shoved ... down: pushed the accelerator with brutality
leaped at: attacked
Alsatian: big guard dog
forgot: did not have in memory • **in gear:** not in neutral
ought to: must • **might :** expresses possibility
hurt: cause a physical pain
brought: guided
spot: place • **banks:** borders • **stream:** river • **left:** placed
by the side: on the border
munched: consumed copiously • **a ... paper:** newspaper
lay: was deposited • **unheeded:** abandoned

'What's the news?' said Edward at last, stretching himself flat on his back and tilting his hat to shade his eyes.

Dorothy glanced over the headlines.

'The Woeful Wife. Extraordinary Story. Twenty-eight People Drowned Last Week. Reported Death of Airman. Startling Jewel Robbery. Ruby Necklace Worth Fifty Thousand Pounds Missing. Oh, Ted! Fifty thousand pounds. Just fancy!' She went on reading. 'The necklace is composed of twenty-one stones set in platinum and was sent by registered post from Paris. On arrival, the packet was found to contain a few pebbles and the jewels were missing.'

'Pinched in the post,' said Edward. 'The posts in France are awful, I believe.'

'I'd like to see a necklace like that,' said Dorothy. 'All glowing like blood – pigeon's blood, that's what they call the colour. I wonder what it would feel like to have a thing like that hanging round your neck.'

'Well, you're never likely to know, my girl,' said Edward facetiously.

Dorothy tossed her head.

'Why not, I should like to know. It's amazing the way girls can get on in the world. I might go on the stage.'

'Girls that behave themselves don't get anywhere,' said Edward discouragingly.

Dorothy opened her mouth to reply, checked herself, and murmured, 'Pass me the cherries.'

'I've been eating more than you have,' she remarked. 'I'll divide up what's left and – why, whatever's this at the bottom of the basket?'

She drew it out as she spoke – a long glittering chain of blood-red stones.

They both stared at it in amazement.

'In the basket, did you say?' said Edward at last.

Dorothy nodded.

'Right at the bottom – under the fruit.'

Again they stared at each other.

'How did it get there, do you think?'

news: fresh information • **stretching...back:** extending his body completely, face upwards • **tilting:** inclining • **shade:** protect
glanced: had a brief look at… • **headlines:** titles
woeful: pathetic
drowned: disappeared in water • **death:** decease • **airman:** pilot
startling: stupefying • **robbery:** illegal capture • **worth:** estimated

fancy: imagine • **went on:** continued • **necklace:** string
stones: precious stones, rubies • **set:** fixed • **registered post:** postal procedure with special precautions
a few: a small number of • **pebbles:** stones of no value • **missing:** absent • **pinched:** taken by fraud (pinch, fam. for steal, rob)
awful: horrible, atrocious • **believe:** think

glowing: scintillating • **blood:** red liquid circulating in arteries and veins • **wonder:** ask myself • **what it...like:** the sensation
hanging: suspended
you're never likely: you have no risk • **know:** know that sensation
facetiously: humorously
tossed: disapproved (with her head)
amazing: extraordinary • **way:** manner
get on: succeed • **in the world:** in life • **go on the stage:** be an actress • **behave themselves:** act correctly • **never get anywhere:** are never successful • **discouragingly:** to discourage her • **checked herself:** stopped suddenly

I've been eating: note progressive form of the perfect
divide up: make two portions • **what's left:** the rest • **bottom:** base
drew it out: pulled the thing out • **glittering:** glowing, shining
blood-red: of the deep red colour of blood
both: the two • **stared:** looked fixedly • **amazement:** stupefaction
at last: after a moment, finally
nodded: approved with her head
right: absolutely

get: arrive • **do you think?:** in your opinion, in your view

'I can't imagine. It's odd, Ted, just after reading that bit in the paper – about the rubies.'

Edward laughed.

'You don't imagine you're holding fifty thousand pounds in your hand, do you?'

'I just said it was odd. Rubies set in platinum. Platinum is that sort of dull silvery stuff – like this. Don't they sparkle and aren't they a lovely colour? I wonder how many of them there are?' She counted. 'I say, Ted, there are twenty-one exactly.'

'No!'

'Yes. The same number as the paper said. Oh, Ted, you don't think –'

'It couldn't be.' But he spoke irresolutely. 'There's some sort of way you can tell – scratching them on glass.'

'That's diamonds. But you know, Ted, that was a very odd-looking man – the man with the fruit – a nasty-looking man. And he was funny about it – said we'd got more than our money's worth in the basket.'

'Yes, but look here, Dorothy. What would he want to hand us over fifty thousand pounds for?'

Miss Pratt shook her head, discouraged.

'It doesn't seem to make sense,' she admitted. 'Unless the police were after him.'

'The police?' Edward paled slightly.

'Yes. It goes on to say in the paper – 'the police have a clue."

Cold shivers ran down Edward's spine.

'I don't like this, Dorothy. Supposing the police get after us.'

Dorothy stared at him with her mouth open.

'But we haven't done anything, Ted. We found it in the basket.'

'And that'll sound a silly sort of story to tell! It isn't likely.'

'It isn't very,' admitted Dorothy. 'Oh, Ted, do you really think it is IT? It's like a fairy story!'

'I don't think it sounds like a fairy story,' said Edward. 'It

odd: strange, bizarre • **bit:** passage
about: concerning
laughed: showed his amusement
you're holding ... hand: you are in possession of

set: inserted
dull: unpolished • **silvery:** grey white • **stuff:** matter • **sparkle:** glow • **lovely:** beautiful • **wonder:** ask myself
I say: expression of surprise • **twenty-one exactly:** Dorothy is beginning to realize that the genuine necklace is in her hands

the same ... as: identical to
think: suppose, imagine
it couldn't be: it is impossible • **irresolutely:** hesitantly
way: method • **tell:** be sure • **scratching ... glass:** grating with firm pression on a mirror, for example • **that's diamonds:** no, that is used for the authentification of diamonds only • **nasty-looking:** very unpleasant • **funny:** strange • **got more ... basket:** we now clearly see why he said that
look here: exclamation to call attention • **hand us over:** pass to us
for: (what…for) why
shook her head: moved her head in a dubious manner
make sense: be comprehensible • **unless:** except if
were after him: in pursuit of the man
slightly: a little
goes on: continues • **the police have:** note the noun treated as plural • **clue:** indication, suspicion
cold shivers ... spine: Edward trembled with terror • **spine:** vertebral column • **after us:** pursue you and me

stared: looked intently; notice "at" • **mouth open:** expression of surprise on her face • **found:** discovered

sound: seem (when we tell it) • **silly:** absurd
likely: probable

fairy: magic, fantastic

sounds to me more like the kind of story where the hero goes to Dartmoor unjustly accused for fourteen years.'

But Dorothy was not listening. She had clasped the necklace round her neck and was judging the effect in a small mirror taken from her handbag.

'The same as a duchess might wear,' she murmured ecstatically.

'I won't believe it,' said Edward violently. 'They're imitation. They must be imitation.'

'Yes, dear,' said Dorothy, still intent on her reflection in the mirror. 'Very likely.'

'Anything else would be too much of a – a coincidence.'

'Pigeon's blood,' murmured Dorothy.

'It's absurd. That's what I say. Absurd. Look here, Dorothy, are you listening to what I say, or are you not?'

Dorothy put away the mirror. She turned to him, one hand on the rubies round her neck.

'How do I look?' she asked.

Edward stared at her, his grievance forgotten. He had never seen Dorothy quite like this. There was a triumph about her, a kind of regal beauty that was completely new to him. The belief that she had jewels round her neck worth fifty thousand pounds had made of Dorothy Pratt a new woman. She looked insolently serene; a kind of Cleopatra and Semiramis and Zenobia rolled into one.

'You look – you look – stunning,' said Edward humbly.

Dorothy laughed, and her laugh, too, was entirely different.

'Look here,' said Edward. 'We've got to do something. We must take them to a police station or something.'

'Nonsense,' said Dorothy. 'You said yourself just now that they wouldn't believe you. You'll probably be sent to prison for stealing them.'

'But – but what else can we do?'

'Keep them,' said the new Dorothy Pratt.

Edward stared at her.

'Keep them? You're mad.'

sounds: appears • **kind:** sort
Dartmoor: notorious prison in Devon • **for:** during
not listening: inattentive • **clasped:** attached

handbag: small bag used by women
the same as: identical to the necklace • **wear:** have on her
ecstatically: with exaltation
won't: (contraction of will not) refuse • **believe**: accept
must be: certainly are
intent on: absorbed in • **reflection:** image
likely: plausible
anything else: another supposition • **too much of a coincidence:** an exaggerated coincidence

put away the mirror: replaced the mirror in her handbag

how do I look?: what impression do I give?
grievance: reproach • **forgotten:** out of his memory
quite: totally
regal beauty: majestic beauty like that of a queen, an empress
belief: conviction
made of: transformed, changed into
Cleopatra and ... Zenobia: queens of Antiquity
rolled into one: amalgamated
stunning: sensational, fantastic
laugh: hilarity, sign of gaiety

we've got to: we have got to, we must (note *got*, familiar use)
them: the rubies • **something:** a thing like that
nonsense: that is stupid • **just now:** a minute before
believe you: be convinced by you
stealing: possessing dishonestly
else: other thing
keep: retain possession of • **new:** transformed, different

mad: completely deranged, mentally unbalanced

'We found them, didn't we? Why should we think they're valuable? We'll keep them and I shall wear them.'

'And the police will pinch you.'

Dorothy considered this for a minute or two.

'All right,' she said. 'We'll sell them. And you can buy a Rolls-Royce, or two Rolls-Royces, and I'll buy a diamond headthing and some rings.'

Still Edward stared. Dorothy showed impatience.

'You've got your chance now – it's up to you to take it. We didn't steal the thing – I wouldn't hold with that. It's come to us and it's probably the only chance we'll ever have of getting all the things we want. Haven't you got any spunk at all, Edward Palgrove?'

Edward found his voice.

'Sell it, you say? That wouldn't be so jolly easy. Any jeweller would want to know where I got the blooming thing.'

'You don't take it to a jeweller. Don't you ever read detective stories, Ted? You take it to a 'fence', of course.'

'And how should I know any fences? I've been brought up respectable.'

'Men ought to know everything,' said Dorothy. 'That's what they're for.'

He looked at her. She was serene and unyielding.

'I wouldn't have believed it of you,' he said weakly.

'I thought you had more spirit.'

There was a pause. Then Dorothy rose to her feet.

'Well,' she said lightly. 'We'd best be getting home.'

'Wearing that thing round your neck?'

Dorothy removed the necklace, looked at it reverently and dropped it into her handbag.

'Look here,' said Edward. 'You give that to me.'

'No.'

'Yes, you do. I've been brought up honest, my girl.'

'Well, you can go on being honest. You need have nothing to do with it.'

'Oh, hand it over,' said Edward recklessly. 'I'll do it. I'll find a fence. As you say, it's the only chance we shall ever have. We came by it honest – bought it for two shillings. It's

should: conditional, what reason have we to think?
shall: future tense usually contracted as in *we'll*
pinch: arrest
considered: meditated on • **for:** in a lapse of time of
buy: obtain in exchange for money

headthing: diadem • **rings:** ornaments for fingers
still: like before • **showed:** manifested signs of
up to you: your responsibility
wouldn't hold with: would not approve of • **it's come:** it has arrived (note the contracted form *it's* for it *has*)
getting: obtaining • **want:** desire • **spunk:** courage and determination
found: recuperated, regained (find, found, found)
not jolly easy: extremely difficult
want: demand • **blooming:** euphemism for "bloody"
take: offer • **ever:** at any time
fence: receiver of stolen goods
brought up: educated

ought to: are supposed to
what they're for: their job
unyielding: resolute
believed it: imagined it • **weakly:** feebly
spirit: courage, energy
rose to her feet: stood up
we'd best be getting: we ought to go (note the expression *had best/better + verb* expressing the best choice to do)
removed: detached • **reverently:** with respect
dropped: let it fall
look here: pay attention to what I am going to say

do: used to refer to a verb already mentioned: *give*
you need have ... with it: your participation is not necessary

hand it over: give it to me • **recklessly:** with temerity

came by: obtained • **honest:** honestly

no more than what gentlemen do in antique shops every day of their life and are proud of it.'

'That's it!' said Dorothy. 'Oh, Edward, you're splendid!'

She handed over the necklace and he dropped it into his pocket. He felt worked up, exalted, the very devil of a fellow! In this mood, he started the Austin. They were both too excited to remember tea. They drove back to London in silence. Once at a crossroads, a policeman stepped towards the car, and Edward's heart missed a beat. By a miracle, they reached home without mishap.

Edward's last words to Dorothy were imbued with the adventurous spirit.

'We'll go through with this. Fifty thousand pounds! It's worth it!'

He dreamt that night of broad arrows and Dartmoor, and rose early, haggard, and unrefreshed. He had to set about finding a fence – and how to do it he had not the remotest idea!

His work at the office was slovenly and brought down upon him two sharp rebukes before lunch.

How did one find a 'fence'? Whitechapel, he fancied, was the correct neighbourhood – or was it Stepney?

On his return to the office a call came through for him on the telephone. Dorothy's voice spoke – tragic and tearful.

'Is that you, Ted? I'm using the telephone, but she may come in any minute, and I'll have to stop. Ted, you haven't done anything, have you?'

Edward replied in the negative.

'Well, look here, Ted, you mustn't. I've been lying awake all night. It's been awful. Thinking of how it says in the Bible you mustn't steal. I must have been mad yesterday – I really must. You won't do anything, will you, Ted, dear?'

Did a feeling of relief steal over Mr Palgrove? Possibly it did – but he wasn't going to admit any such thing.

'When I say I'm going through with a thing, I go through with it,' he said in a voice such as might belong to a strong superman with eyes of steel.

'Oh, but, Ted, dear, you mustn't. Oh, Lord, she's coming.

no more: not more dishonest • **gentlemen ... shops:** antiquarians practise • **proud of:** very satisfied with
that's it: exactly, that is an excellent argument
dropped: put, let fall
felt worked up: had a sense of excitement • **the very devil of a fellow:** a man of genius • **mood:** state of mind
drove back: returned
crossroads: intersection of two roads • **stepped:** moved
missed a beat: stopped for a moment
reached: attained • **mishap:** difficulty, problem
imbued: penetrated (note *with*)

go through: complete, conclude, finish • **this:** this affair
worth it: sufficiently important
dreamt: hallucinated • **broad arrows:** marks of prisoners
rose: came out of bed • **unrefreshed:** fatigued • **set about:** begin
do it: not to repeat "find a fence" • **remotest:** vaguest (superlative of vague)
office: professional place • **slovenly:** negligent • **brought ... him:** caused to him • **sharp rebukes:** acid remarks
fancied: imagined
neighbourhood: district
a call ... telephone: he had a telephone call
tearful: emotional
she: the "old cat"
any minute: now or later
done anything: put our project into action
replied in the negative: gave a negative answer, said no
lying awake: not sleeping
awful: terrible, horrid • **says:** is written
must have been: have certainly been (must + present perfect: possibility or obligation in the past)
feeling of relief: sensation of deliverance • **steal over:** invade him
any such thing: a thing like that, that sensation

belong: be possessed by • **steel:** hard strong grey metal

Lord: exclamation of irritation

Look here, Ted, she's going out to dinner tonight. I can slip out and meet you. Don't do anything till you've seen me. Eight o'clock. Wait for me round the corner.' Her voice changed to a seraphic murmur. 'Yes, ma'am, I think it was a wrong number. It was Bloomsbury 0243 they wanted.'

As Edward left the office at six o'clock, a huge headline caught his eye.

JEWEL ROBBERY
LATEST DEVELOPMENTS

Hurriedly he extended a penny. Safely ensconced in the tube, having dexterously managed to gain a seat, he eagerly perused the printed sheet. He found what he sought easily enough.

A suppressed whistle escaped him.

'Well – I'm –'

And then another adjacent paragraph caught his eye. He read it through and let the paper slip to the floor unheeded.

Precisely at eight o'clock, he was waiting at the rendezvous. A breathless Dorothy, looking pale but pretty, came hurrying along to join him.

'You haven't done anything, Ted?'

'I haven't done anything.' He took the ruby chain from his pocket. 'You can put it on.'

'But, Ted –'

'The police have got the rubies all right – and the man who pinched them. And now read this!'

He thrust a newspaper paragraph under her nose. Dorothy read:

NEW ADVERTISING STUNT

A clever new advertising dodge is being adopted by the All-English Fivepenny Fair who intend to challenge the famous Woolworth's. Baskets of fruit were sold yesterday and will be on sale every Sunday. Out of every fifty baskets, one will contain an imitation necklace in different coloured stones. These necklaces are really wonderful value for the money.

going out: invited • **slip out:** go out furtively
and meet: to see (note "and" before the verb indicating intention)
wait for me: don't move until I arrive
seraphic: celestial • **ma'am:** Madam, talking to her employer
wrong: incorrect • **number:** telephone number
huge: enormous, immense • **headline:** announcing the article
caught his eye: attracted his attention

latest developments: fresh news

hurriedly: with precipitation • **extended:** gave • **ensconced:** protected
tube: metro in London • **managed ... seat:** sat down • **eagerly perused:** examined with avidity • **sheet:** page • **sought:** wanted to read • **enough:** relatively (note place of *enough* after the adverb)
suppressed whistle: repressed noise of surprise

he read it through: from the first line to the last, entirely
slip: fall • **unheeded:** negligently

breathless: respiring with difficulty • **pretty:** charming • **came along:** approached • **hurrying:** in haste

put it on: put it on your neck, wear it

all right: without difficulty, in a satisfactory manner
pinched: stole (steal, stole, stolen)
thrust: pushed violently • **under her nose:** in her face

advertising stunt: spectacular action as publicity
dodge: stunt • **All-English ... Fair:** festival organized in favour of English products • **intend to:** cf intention • **challenge:** defy
Woolworth's: the Fair organized by Woolworth
out of...baskets: in a series of fifty baskets • **one:** one only
imitation: not authentic, not genuine!
wonderful: extraordinary, marvellous

Great excitement and merriment was caused by them yesterday and EAT MORE FRUIT will have a great vogue next Sunday. We congratulate the Fivepenny Fair on their resource and wish them all good luck in their campaign of Buy British Goods.

'Well –' said Dorothy.

And after a pause: 'Well!'

'Yes,' said Edward. 'I felt the same.'

A passing man thrust a paper into his hand.

'Take one, brother,' he said.

'The price of a virtuous woman is far above rubies.'

'There!' said Edward. 'I hope that cheers you up.'

'I don't know,' said Dorothy doubtfully. 'I don't exactly want to *look* like a good woman.'

'You don't,' said Edward. 'That's why the man gave me that paper. With those rubies round your neck you don't look one little bit like a good woman.'

Dorothy laughed.

'You're rather a dear, Ted,' she said. 'Come on, let's go to the pictures.'

excitement: enthusiasm • **merriment:** hilarity, amusement
vogue: popularity
congratulate: felicitate • **resource:** invention, strategy
good luck: satisfaction • **goods:** merchandise

well: exclamation to express her resignation

felt the same: had the same reaction
thrust: put brusquely
brother: dear friend, as if of the same religion
far above: infinitely superior to
there: expresses satisfaction • **hope:** wish • **cheers you up:** consoles you • **doubtfully:** with uncertainty
look like: have the appearance of, resemble
that's why: it is because (the reason why) you look not respectable
not...one little bit: not at all, not in the least
good woman: respectable

rather a dear: really a sweet, charming boy
the pictures: the cinema, the movies

While the Light Lasts

The Ford car bumped from rut to rut, and the hot African sun poured down unmercifully. On either side of the so-called road stretched an unbroken line of trees and scrub, rising and falling in gently undulating lines as far as the eye could reach, the colouring a soft, deep yellow-green, the whole effect languorous and strangely quiet. Few birds stirred the slumbering silence. Once a snake wriggled across the road in front of the car, escaping the driver's efforts at destruction with sinuous ease. Once a native stepped out from the bush, dignified and upright, behind him a woman with an infant bound closely to her broad back and a complete household equipment, including a frying pan, balanced magnificently on her head.

All these things George Crozier had not failed to point out to his wife, who had answered him with a monosyllabic lack of attention which irritated him.

'Thinking of that fellow,' he deduced wrathfully. It was thus that he was wont to allude in his own mind to Deirdre Crozier's first husband, killed in the first year of the War. Killed, too, in the campaign against German West Africa. Natural she should, perhaps – he stole a glance at her, her fairness, the pink and white smoothness of her cheek; the rounded lines of her figure – rather more rounded perhaps than they had been in those far-off days when she had passively permitted him to become engaged to her, and then, in that first emotional scare of war, had abruptly cast him aside and made a war wedding of it with that lean, sunburnt boy lover of hers, Tim Nugent.

Well, well, the fellow was dead – gallantly dead – and he, George Crozier, had married the girl he had always meant to marry. She was fond of him, too; how could she help it when he was ready to gratify her every wish and had the money to do it, too! He reflected with some complacency on his

bumped: made sudden movements • **rut:** profound mark
poured...unmercifully: burnt violently • **either...:** the two sides
stretched: extended • **unbroken:** continuous • **scrub:** trees and plants • **gently:** moderately • **as far ... reached:** to the horizon
the colouring: its colour being • **deep** ≠ pale • **whole:** entire
few: a small number of • **stirred:** troubled • **slumbering:** calm
once: one time • **snake:** serpent • **wriggled across:** zigzagged from one side of the road to the other • **driver:** motorist
ease: facility • **stepped out:** came out • **bush:** small trees
upright ≠ curved, bent • **behind** ≠ in front of • **bound closely:** attached firmly • **broad:** big, wide • **household equipment:** utensils necessary to the house • **frying pan:** *poêle à frire*
had not failed: did not omit • **point out:** indicate
lack of: absence of

fellow: man • **deduced:** concluded • **wrathfully:** furiously
thus: in this manner • **wont:** accustomed • **allude:** refer • **in his own mind:** in his head, in his thoughts (*own* is used to reinforce *his*)
too: not only killed, but killed in Africa
natural she should: naturally she thought of him • **stole a glance:** looked secretly • **fairness:** beauty • **smoothness:** delicate texture
figure: form of the body • **rather:** to a certain degree
those: plural of "that" • **far-off:** distant, past
engaged to her: her fiancé; engaged to be married
scare: fear, sense of danger • **cast aside:** rejected
wedding: marriage ceremony • **lean:** not fat, thin • **that ... lover of hers:** that...lover she had
dead ≠ living • **gallantly:** courageously
meant: intended, desired
was fond of: felt affection for • **too:** as well • **help it:** resist
ready: prepared • **gratify:** satisfy • **every wish:** all her desires
some complacency: a certain amount of satisfaction

last gift to her, at Kimberley, where, owing to his friendship with some of the directors of De Beers, he had been able to purchase a diamond which, in the ordinary way, would not have been in the market, a stone not remarkable as to size, but of a very exquisite and rare shade, a peculiar deep amber, almost old gold, a diamond such as you might not find in a hundred years. And the look in her eyes when he gave it to her! Women were all the same about diamonds.

The necessity of holding on with both hands to prevent himself being jerked out brought George Crozier back to the realities. He cried out for perhaps the fourteenth time, with the pardonable irritation of a man who owns two Rolls Royce cars and who has exercised his stud on the highways of civilization: 'Good Lord, what a car! What a road!' He went on angrily: 'Where the devil is this tobacco estate, anyway? It's over an hour since we left Bulawayo.'

'Lost in Rhodesia,' said Deirdre lightly between two involuntary leaps into the air.

But the coffee-coloured driver, appealed to, responded with the cheering news that their destination was just round the next bend of the road.

The manager of the estate, Mr Walters, was waiting on the step to receive them with the touch of deference due to George Crozier's prominence in Union Tobacco. He introduced his daughter-in-law, who shepherded Deirdre through the cool, dark inner hall to a bedroom beyond, where she could remove the veil with which she was always careful to shield her complexion when motoring. As she unfastened the pins in her usual leisurely, graceful fashion, Deirdre's eyes swept round the whitewashed ugliness of the bare room. No luxuries here, and Deirdre, who loved comfort as a cat loves cream, shivered a little. On the wall a text confronted her. 'What shall it profit a man if he gain the whole world and lose his own soul?' it demanded of all and sundry, and Deirdre, pleasantly conscious that the question had nothing to do with her, turned to accompany her shy and rather silent guide. She noted, but not in the least maliciously, the spreading hips

last ≠ first • **gift:** sth offered • **owing to:** because of
De Beers: famous company exploiting the diamond mines of Kimberley in South Africa • **purchase:** acquire, buy
stone: precious stone • **as to size:** considering its dimension
exquisite: magnificent • **shade:** colour • **peculiar:** rare
almost: practically • **such as:** of the sort that • **might:** expresses possibility
all the same: identical • **about diamonds:** when diamonds are concerned • **holding on:** sitting firmly • **prevent:** avoid, stop
jerked out: ejected • **brought ... back:** caused him to return
cried out: exclaimed • **perhaps:** probably
owns: possesses, has
exercised: practised • **his stud:** his 2 cars • **highways:** good large roads • **went on:** continued • **estate:** property
angrily: furiously, with anger • **where ... is:** emphatic for where is
over: more than • **since:** from the time when • **left:** quitted
Rhodesia: now Zimbabwe • **lightly:** frivolously
leaps: sudden movements, jumps
appealed to: Crozier's comment was addressed to the driver
cheering: encouraging • **news:** new information • **round:** on the other side of • **the next bend:** the first curve they will see

waiting: standing patiently to meet them
step: doorstep, entrance
prominence: importance
daughter-in-law: son's wife • **shepherded:** guided ... along
cool: pleasantly cold • **inner:** interior • **beyond:** on the other side
remove: take off • **careful:** attentive
shield: protect • **unfastened:** opened • **pins:** clips to maintain her veil • **leisurely:** relaxed • **fashion:** manner
swept round: examined • **whitewashed:** painted white • **ugliness** ≠ beauty • **bare** ≠ decorated
shivered: trembled • **confronted her:** attracted her eyes
gain: conquer • **world:** universe • **lose** ≠ gain
soul: immaterial part of a man • **all and sundry:** everyone
had nothing to do with her: she was not concerned
shy: timid • **noted:** remarked • **but not ... maliciously:** with no bad intention at all • **spreading hips:** big posterior!

and the unbecoming cheap cotton gown. And with a glow of quiet appreciation her eyes dropped to the exquisite, costly simplicity of her own French white linen. Beautiful clothes, especially when worn by herself, roused in her the joy of the artist.

The two men were waiting for her.

'It won't bore you to come round, too, Mrs Crozier?'

'Not at all. I've never been over a tobacco factory.'

They stepped out into the still Rhodesian afternoon.

'These are the seedlings here; we plant them out as required. You see –'

The manager's voice droned on, interpolated by her husband's sharp staccato questions – output, stamp duty, problems of coloured labour. She ceased to listen.

This was Rhodesia, this was the land Tim had loved, where he and she were to have gone together after the War was over. If he had not been killed! As always, the bitterness of revolt surged up in her at that thought. Two short months – that was all they had had. Two months of happiness – if that mingled rapture and pain were happiness. Was love ever happiness? Did not a thousand tortures beset the lover's heart? She had lived intensely in that short space, but had she ever known the peace, the leisure, the quiet contentment of her present life? And for the first time she admitted, somewhat unwillingly, that perhaps all had been for the best.

'I wouldn't have liked living out here. I mightn't have been able to make Tim happy. I might have disappointed him. George loves me, and I'm very fond of him, and he's very, very good to me. Why, look at that diamond he bought me only the other day.' And, thinking of it, her eyelids drooped a little in pure pleasure.

'This is where we thread the leaves.' Walters led the way into a low, long shed. On the floor were vast heaps of green leaves, and white-clad black 'boys' squatted round them, picking and rejecting with deft fingers, sorting them into sizes, and stringing them by means of primitive needles on a long line of string. They worked with a cheerful leisureliness,

unbecoming: not flattering • **cheap:** of no value • **glow ...**
appreciation: interior sense of satisfaction • **dropped:** came down
clothes: a dress, a shirt, a pull-over are clothes
worn by herself: had on her • **roused:** produced, raised

won't: will not • **bore** ≠ interest • **come round:** visit the place

been over: visited, seen • **factory:** building where tobacco is treated • **into:** entering • **still:** calm

seedlings: young plants • **plant ... required:** replant when new adult plants are necessary

droned on: continued in a monotonous tone • **interpolated:** interrupted • **sharp:** incisive • **output:** production • **stamp duty:** tax • **coloured labour:** black workers • **listen:** pay attention to what was said • **land:** country
were ... gone: had decided to go • **together:** he & she • **over:** ended • **killed** ≠ living • **as always:** like usually • **bitterness:** resentment, sense of injustice • **surged up:** appeared suddenly
happiness: felicity • **mingled:** mixed
rapture: great joy • **ever:** always (used in questions)
thousand: 1,000, a great number • **beset:** assail • **heart:** centre of sentiments • **short** ≠ long
leisure: time when you don't work • **quiet:** untroubled, calm
somewhat: a little • **unwillingly:** not voluntarily, in spite of herself
for the best: good in the end

wouldn't: didn't want to • **mightn't ... able:** probably was not capable • **might:** used for probability • **disappointed him:** not satisfied his expectations
why: emphatic exclamation • **bought:** acquired, purchased
only ... day: just some days before • **her eyelids drooped:** she shut her eyes

thread: put on a line • **led...into:** directed them to enter
shed: simple covered structure • **heaps:** piles
white-clad: dressed in white • **squatted:** seated on the floor
picking: choosing • **deft:** adroit • **sorting:** arranging
stringing: attaching • **by means of:** using • **needles:** *aiguilles*
string: thin cord • **cheerful:** gay • **leisureliness** ≠ precipitation

jesting amongst themselves, and showing their white teeth as they laughed.

'Now, out here –'

They passed through the shed into the daylight again, where the lines of leaves hung drying in the sun. Deirdre sniffed delicately at the faint, almost imperceptible fragrance that filled the air.

Walters led the way into other sheds where the tobacco, kissed by the sun into faint yellow discoloration, underwent its further treatment. Dark here, with the brown swinging masses above, ready to fall to powder at a rough touch. The fragrance was stronger, almost overpowering it seemed to Deirdre, and suddenly a sort of terror came upon her, a fear of she knew not what, that drove her from that menacing, scented obscurity out into the sunlight. Crozier noted her pallor.

'What's the matter, my dear, don't you feel well? The sun, perhaps. Better not come with us round the plantations? Eh?'

Walters was solicitous. Mrs Crozier had better go back to the house and rest. He called to a man a little distance away.

'Mr Arden – Mrs Crozier. Mrs Crozier's feeling a little done up with the heat, Arden. Just take her back to the house, will you?'

The momentary feeling of dizziness was passing. Deirdre walked by Arden's side. She had as yet hardly glanced at him.

'Deirdre!'

Her heart gave a leap, and then stood still. Only one person had ever spoken her name like that, with the faint stress on the first syllable that made of it a caress.

She turned and stared at the man by her side. He was burnt almost black by the sun, he walked with a limp, and on the cheek nearer hers was a long scar which altered his expression, but she knew him.

'Tim!'

For an eternity, it seemed to her, they gazed at each other, mute and trembling, and then, without knowing how or why,

jesting: saying humorous things • **amongst themselves:** in their group • **laughed:** expressed amusement, hilarity
out here: end of the visit (to continue the visit)
passed through: moved along • **into:** entering
hung: were suspended • **drying:** become dry ≠ wet, full of water
sniffed: inhaled • **faint:** delicate • **fragrance:** pleasant odour
filled: invaded
led the way: guided them
kissed: gently touched • **underwent:** was subjected to
further: additional • **swinging:** suspended and moving
fall to powder: be pulverized • **rough:** brusque
stronger: more important • **overpowering:** too intense
came upon: seized • **fear:** sense of danger, fright
drove her from ... out into: forced her to go out of the shed
scented: perfumed • **sunlight** ≠ obscurity • **noted:** observed

matter: problem • **don't you feel well?:** are you all right?
better: (it is) preferable (that you) • **come ... round:** visit

solicitous: anxious, full of solicitude • **had better:** it would be prudent for her to • **rest:** be quiet • **called to:** spoke to
away: from the place where they were
Mrs C's feeling: Mrs C. is feeling, has the sensation of being
done up: extremely fatigued • **heat** ≠ cold • **take her back:** make her return • **will you?:** please
dizziness: vertigo
by...side: near • **as yet:** up to now • **hardly:** just • **glanced:** looked momentarily
gave a leap: beat suddenly • **stood still:** stopped beating
ever: at any time • **spoken:** pronounced • **faint stress:** delicate accent • **made of it:** transformed it into
stared: looked fixedly
burnt: extremely tanned • **with a limp:** with one leg moving less well • **cheek:** part of the face under the eye • **scar:** mark on his face, cicatrix
Tim!: she recognizes him
gazed: looked intently • **at each other:** with reciprocity
mute: silent • **how or why:** manner or reason

they were in each other's arms. Time rolled back for them. Then they drew apart again, and Deirdre, conscious as she put it of the idiocy of the question, said:

'Then you're not dead?'

'No, they must have mistaken another chap for me. I was badly knocked on the head, but I came to and managed to crawl into the bush. After that I don't know what happened for months and months, but a friendly tribe looked after me, and at last I got my proper wits again and managed to get back to civilization.' He paused. 'I found you'd been married six months.'

Deirdre cried out:

'Oh, Tim, understand, please understand! It was so awful, the loneliness – and the poverty. I didn't mind being poor with you, but when I was alone I hadn't the nerve to stand up against the sordidness of it all.'

'It's all right, Deirdre; I did understand. I know you always have had a hankering after the flesh-pots. I took you from them once – but the second time, well – my nerve failed. I was pretty badly broken up, you see, could hardly walk without a crutch, and then there was this scar.'

She interrupted him passionately.

'Do you think I would have cared for that?'

'No, I know you wouldn't. I was a fool. Some women did mind, you know. I made up my mind I'd manage to get a glimpse of you. If you looked happy, if I thought you were contented to be with Crozier – why, then I'd remain dead. I did see you. You were just getting into a big car. You had on some lovely sable furs – things I'd never be able to give you if I worked my fingers to the bone – and – well – you seemed happy enough. I hadn't the same strength and courage, the same belief in myself, that I'd had before the War. All I could see was myself, broken and useless, barely able to earn enough to keep you – and you looked so beautiful, Deirdre, such a queen amongst women, so worthy to have furs and jewels and lovely clothes and all the hundred and one luxuries Crozier could give you. That – and – well, the

were ... arms: embraced • **time ... back:** the past returned
drew apart: separated • **again:** as they were before • **as she put it:** at the moment she asked

then: apparently

mistaken: incorrectly identified • **chap:** fellow, man
badly: severely • **knocked:** mutilated • **came to:** recovered consciousness • **crawl:** move like a snake • **happened:** took place
for: during • **looked after:** protected and saved
at last: finally • **got ... wits:** became conscious • **managed to:** succeeded in • **get back:** return • **paused:** stopped • **found:** discovered • **six months:** for six months

understand: be comprehensive • **awful:** horrible
loneliness: solitude • **mind:** regard as important
alone: with no one • **nerve:** courage • **stand up against:** be combative, fight

all right: ok • **did understand:** emphatic form for understood
had ... after: desired profoundly • **flesh-pots:** luxurious places • **I... from them:** forced you to abandon • **failed:** left me
pretty: very • **broken up:** depressed • **hardly:** practically not
crutch: cane to help walking • **scar:** mark left after his accident

would have: past conditional • **cared for:** attached importance

a fool: stupid • **some:** a certain number of
did mind: (emphatic) cared • **made ... mind:** decided • **get:** obtain • **glimpse:** quick view • **looked:** seemed
contented: satisfied • **remain dead:** do nothing as if dead

lovely: nice • **sable furs:** coats made of black marten • **never** ≠ always • **worked ... bone:** (idiomatic) worked as hard as possible
enough: moderately • **strength:** physical force
same ≠ different • **belief:** self-assurance, confidence
broken: destroyed • **useless:** incompetent, of no use
earn: gain money • **enough:** sufficiently • **keep you:** maintain you
amongst: in a group of • **so worthy:** greatly meriting
jewels: precious personal ornaments
luxuries: costly things, jewels, furs, etc.

pain – of seeing you together, decided me. Everyone believed me dead. I would stay dead.'

'The pain!' repeated Deirdre in a low voice.

'Well, damn it all, Deirdre, it hurt! It isn't that I blame you. I don't. But it hurt.'

They were both silent. Then Tim raised her face to his and kissed it with a new tenderness.

'But that's all over now, sweetheart. The only thing to decide is how we're going to break it to Crozier.'

'Oh!' She drew herself away abruptly. 'I hadn't thought –' She broke off as Crozier and the manager appeared round the angle of the path. With a swift turn of the head she whispered:

'Do nothing now. Leave it to me. I must prepare him. Where could I meet you tomorrow?'

Nugent reflected.

'I could come in to Bulawayo. How about the Café near the Standard Bank? At three o'clock it would be pretty empty.'

Deirdre gave a brief nod of assent before turning her back on him and joining the other two men. Tim Nugent looked after her with a faint frown. Something in her manner puzzled him.

Deirdre was very silent during the drive home. Sheltering behind the fiction of a 'touch of the sun', she deliberated on her course of action. How should she tell him? How would he take it? A strange lassitude seemed to possess her, and a growing desire to postpone the revelation as long as might be. Tomorrow would be soon enough. There would be plenty of time before three o'clock.

The hotel was uncomfortable. Their room was on the ground floor, looking out on to an inner court. Deirdre stood that evening sniffing the stale air and glancing distastefully at the tawdry furniture. Her mind flew to the easy luxury of Monkton Court amidst the Surrey pinewoods. When her maid left her at last, she went slowly to her jewel case. In the palm of her hand the golden diamond returned her stare.

together: you and him • **believed ... dead:** thought, considered I was dead • **would:** wanted to, chose to • **stay:** continue to be
pain: suffering • **low** ≠ high
damn it all: exclamation expressing frustration • **hurt:** made suffer
both: the two • **raised:** lifted • **to his:** near his face

over: finished • **sweetheart:** darling, my dear • **only:** unique
how: in what manner • **we're going to:** we will • **break:** announce
drew herself away: drew apart, separated from him
broke off: stopped talking • **as:** just when • **round:** at
path: alley • **swift:** quick, rapid
whispered: murmured, spoke in a low voice
now: at present • **leave it to me:** let me do it
could: possibility • **meet:** see • **tomorrow:** next day

come in: go • **how about:** what do you think of meeting at
would: probably • **pretty:** practically, quite • **empty:** no one there ≠ full • **nod:** movement of the head • **assent:** approval • **turning her back on him:** turning away from him
looked after her: continued to look at her • **frown:** grimace
puzzled him: made him uncertain

during the ... home: as they returned home by car • **sheltering behind:** protecting herself by using • **deliberated on:** considered
should: obligation in the conditional • **would:** was going to (anticipation) • **take:** accept, receive
growing: developing • **postpone:** adjourn, delay • **might be:** possible • **soon enough:** the right time • **plenty of:** much

on the ground floor ... court: with direct access to an enclosed space
stood: not wanting to sit down • **stale** ≠ fresh • **distastefully:** with disgust • **tawdry:** sordid • **furniture:** table, chairs, etc. • **flew:** turned back • **amidst:** in the middle of • **Surrey:** in South England • **maid:** servant • **slowly** ≠ rapidly
case: box • **golden:** the colour of gold • **returned:** reflected

With an almost violent gesture she returned it to the case and slammed down the lid. Tomorrow morning she would tell George.

She slept badly. It was stifling beneath the heavy folds of the mosquito netting. The throbbing darkness was punctuated by the ubiquitous *ping* she had learnt to dread. She awoke white and listless. Impossible to start a scene so early in the day!

She lay in the small, close room all the morning, resting. Lunchtime came upon her with a sense of shock. As they sat drinking coffee, George Crozier proposed a drive to the Matopos.

'Plenty of time if we start at once.'

Deirdre shook her head, pleading a headache, and she thought to herself: 'That settles it. I can't rush the thing. After all, what does a day more or less matter? I'll explain to Tim.'

She waved goodbye to Crozier as he rattled off in the battered Ford. Then, glancing at her watch, she walked slowly to the meeting place.

The Café was deserted at this hour. They sat down at a little table and ordered the inevitable tea that South Africa drinks at all hours of the day and night. Neither of them said a word till the waitress brought it and withdrew to her fastness behind some pink curtains. Then Deirdre looked up and started as she met the intense watchfulness in his eyes.

'Deirdre, have you told him?'

She shook her head, moistening her lips, seeking for words that would not come.

'Why not?'

'I haven't had a chance; there hasn't been time.'

Even to herself the words sounded halting and unconvincing.

'It's not that. There's something else. I suspected it yesterday. I'm sure of it today. Deirdre, what is it?'

She shook her head dumbly.

'There's some reason why you don't want to leave George

almost: rather • **returned:** placed it back
slammed down: shut violently • **lid:** cover, top
tell: speak to, break to
stifling: oppressive • **beneath ... netting:** under the thick material used against mosquitos • **throbbing:** palpitating
ubiquitous: omnipresent • **dread:** apprehend • **awoke** ≠ slept
listless: languid • **start:** begin • **scene:** quarrel • **early** ≠ late

lay: stayed in bed • **close:** suffocating, stale
came upon: fell on • **as:** when, during the time when
proposed a drive: offered to go by car
Matopos: National Park in Zimbabwe (ex Rhodesia)
plenty of: ample • **start:** go, move • **at once:** immediately
shook her head ≠ nodded to refuse • **pleading:** giving the pretext of • **settles:** resolves • **rush the thing:** precipitate the news
what does ... matter?: is it important if it is today or tomorrow?

waved: moved her hand to say • **rattled off:** left with a great noise
battered: decrepit • **at her watch:** to see the time
meeting place: rendez-vous
deserted: empty

neither of them: not Deirdre and not Tim
till: up to the moment when • **waitress:** server • **withdrew ... fastness:** went to her refuge • **pink:** rose-coloured
started: had a movement of surprise • **met:** encountered
watchfulness: intense attention
moistening: humidifying, she had no saliva • **seeking for ... come:** try to speak in vain

chance: opportunity • **time:** enough, sufficient time
even: not only to Tim but also to her • **sounded halting:** seemed hesitating
that: a question of time • **something else:** another cause

dumbly: unable to speak
some: a certain • **leave:** abandon

Crozier, why you don't want to come back to me. What is it?'

It was true. As he said it she knew it, knew it with sudden scorching shame, but knew it beyond any possibility of doubt. And still his eyes searched her.

'It isn't that you love him! You don't. But there's something.'

She thought: 'In another moment he'll see! Oh, God, don't let him!'

Suddenly his face whitened.

'Deirdre – is it – is it that there's going to be a – child?'

In a flash she saw the chance he offered her. A wonderful way! Slowly, almost without her own volition, she bowed her head.

She heard his quick breathing, then his voice, rather high and hard.

'That – alters things. I didn't know. We've got to find a different way out.' He leant across the table and caught both her hands in his. 'Deirdre, my darling, never think – never dream that you were in any way to blame. Whatever happens, remember that. I should have claimed you when I came back to England. I funked it, so it's up to me to do what I can to put things straight now. You see? Whatever happens, don't fret, darling. Nothing has been your fault.'

He lifted first one hand, then the other to his lips. Then she was alone, staring at the untasted tea. And, strangely enough, it was only one thing that she saw – a gaudily illuminated text hanging on a whitewashed wall. The words seemed to spring out from it and hurl themselves at her. 'What shall it profit a man –' She got up, paid for her tea and went out.

On his return George Crozier was met by a request that his wife might not be disturbed. Her headache, the maid said, was very bad.

It was nine o'clock the next morning when he entered her bedroom, his face rather grave. Deirdre was sitting up in bed. She looked white and haggard, but her eyes shone.

'George, I've got something to tell you, something rather terrible –'

want: desire (note insistance: you don't want) • **come back to:** live with
true: right ≠ false, wrong • **as:** just at the moment when
scorching: intense • **shame** ≠ self-esteem • **beyond:** without
still: like before • **searched her:** tried to see her face, to understand • **don't:** don't love him
something: a reason you don't want to reveal
see: understand • **don't let him:** how I desire that he will not see

whitened: became pale, livid
there's going ... child: (near future) you're going to have a baby
in a flash: in no time, in a second • **wonderful:** marvelous
way: solution • **without ... volition:** involuntarily • **bowed:** inclined

quick breathing: rapid respiration • **rather:** very • **high** ≠ low
hard: unpleasant, not gentle
alters things: changes the situation
a ... way out: another solution • **leant across:** inclined himself on
caught: seized • **his:** his hands • **think:** imperative form
dream: imagine • **in any way:** in some degree • **whatever happens:** in all circumstances • **claimed:** regained
funked: eluded, avoided • **it's up to me:** it depends on me
straight: in order
fret: be anxious and nervous

alone: he had left • **untasted:** untouched • **strangely:** curiously
gaudily illuminated: decorated in very bright colours
hanging: suspended • **spring out from it:** detach themselves suddenly from the wall • **hurl themselves:** rush • **what shall ... man:** (prophetic future) cf Bible, Mark 8,36 • **got up** ≠ sat down
was met: was received • **request:** demand
might: for permission • **disturbed:** troubled • **headache:** pain in her head
entered: note no preposition
sitting up ≠ lying
looked: appeared, seemed • **shone:** were bright, clear
I've got: familiar for I have • **rather:** absolutely

He interrupted her brusquely.

'So you've heard. I was afraid it might upset you.'

'Upset me?'

'Yes. You talked to the poor young fellow that day.'

He saw her hand steal to her heart, her eyelids flicker, then she said in a low, quick voice that somehow frightened him:

'I've heard nothing. Tell me quickly.'

'I thought –'

'Tell me!'

'Out at that tobacco estate. Chap shot himself. Badly broken up in the War, nerves all to pieces, I suppose. There's no other reason to account for it.'

'He shot himself – in that dark shed where the tobacco was hanging.' She spoke with certainty, her eyes like a sleep-walker's as she saw before her in the odorous darkness a figure lying there, revolver in hand.

'Why, to be sure; that's where you were taken queer yesterday. Odd thing, that!'

Deirdre did not answer. She saw another picture – a table with tea things on it, and a woman bowing her head in acceptance of a lie.

'Well, well, the War has a lot to answer for,' said Crozier, and stretched out his hand for a match, lighting his pipe with careful puffs.

His wife's cry startled him.

'Ah! don't, don't! I can't bear the smell!'

He stared at her in kindly astonishment.

'My dear girl, you mustn't be nervy. After all, you can't escape from the smell of tobacco. You'll meet it everywhere.'

'Yes, everywhere!' She smiled a slow, twisted smile, and murmured some words that he did not catch, words that she had chosen for the original obituary notice of Tim Nugent's death. 'While the light lasts I shall remember, and in the darkness I shall not forget.'

Her eyes widened as they followed the ascending spiral of smoke, and she repeated in a low, monotonous voice: 'Everywhere, everywhere.'

you've heard: you know the news • **was afraid:** feared, apprehended that • **upset:** disturb, distress
fellow: boy • **that day:** the day sth happened
steal: move furtively • **her eyelids flicker:** she opened and shut her eyes rapidly • **somehow:** in a certain degree • **frightened:** made him anxious, gave him a feeling of fear

out: not in town • **shot himself:** committed suicide with a revolver
broken up: prostrated • **all to pieces:** in poor condition
account for it: justify it, explain it
dark: obscure
like a sleepwalker's: like the eyes of a sleepwalker, a person walking in his sleep • **she saw ...:** she imagined the scene
figure: body • **lying:** extended on the ground
to be sure: exactly • **where ... queer:** where she didn't feel well • **odd thing:** a strange circumstance • **that:** the fact that it happened at the same place, in the shed • **picture:** scene, image

lie: sth which does not exist, not true
has a lot to answer for: is responsible for many things
stretched out ... for: took a match in a box • **lighting:** making burn
with careful puffs: delicately smoking
startled: started, shocked
don't: don't smoke • **bear:** tolerate, endure • **smell:** odour
kindly: gentle
nervy: nervous, alarmed
escape from: evade from, avoid
everywhere: in every part of this country
twisted smile: rictus
catch: seize, understand
chosen: selected • **original:** first • **obituary notice:** death announcement • **while:** during the time when • **lasts:** goes on, continues • **shall:** emphatic future • **forget** ≠ remember, keep in memory • **widened:** dilated • **followed:** moved along

everywhere: in her and around her

The Case of the Caretaker

'Well,' demanded Doctor Haydock of his patient. 'And how goes it today?'

Miss Marple smiled at him wanly from pillows.

'I suppose, really, that I'm better,' she admitted, 'but I feel so terribly depressed. I can't help feeling how much better it would have been if I had died. After all, I'm an old woman. Nobody wants me or cares about me.'

Doctor Haydock interrupted with his usual brusqueness. 'Yes, yes, typical after-reaction of this type of flu. What you need is something to take you out of yourself. A mental tonic.'

Miss Marple sighed and shook her head.

'And what's more,' continued Doctor Haydock, 'I've brought my medicine with me!'

He tossed a long envelope on to the bed.

'Just the thing for you. The kind of puzzle that is right up your street.'

'A puzzle?' Miss Marple looked interested.

'Literary effort of mine,' said the doctor, blushing a little. 'Tried to make a regular story of it. "He said," "she said," "the girl thought," etc. Facts of the story are true.'

'But why a puzzle?' asked Miss Marple.

Doctor Haydock grinned. 'Because the interpretation is up to you. I want to see if you're as clever as you always make out.'

With that Parthian shot he departed.

Miss Marple picked up the manuscript and began to read.

'And where is the bride?' asked Miss Harmon genially.

The village was all agog to see the rich and beautiful young wife that Harry Laxton had brought back from abroad. There

well: introduces a question • **how goes it?:** how are you, how do you feel?

wanly: feebly • **from:** with her head on • **pillows:** soft supports for her head in bed • **I feel:** think I am, I am conscious of being

can't help: can't stop (+ -ing) • **better:** preferable

would have been: past conditional • **died:** deceased

wants me: desires my presence • **or:** and nobody • **cares about:** has affection for

flu: influenza, grippe • **what you need:** what is necessary to you

take you ... yourself: interest you in something

sighed: exhaled plaintively • **shook her head:** moved her head in refusal

brought: come here with • **medecine:** remedy

tossed: let fall, threw • **to:** indicates movement

the thing for you: what you need • **right up your street:** (informal) well-adapted to your ability, to your talent

looked: seemed • **puzzle:** enigma, mystery

literary ... of mine: my literary effort • **blushing:** become red in the face • **tried:** essayed, attempted • **regular:** veritable

true: real

grinned: smiled happily, with gaity • **is up to:** depends on

as clever as ... make out: extremely talented, intelligent like you always pretend

Parthian shot: last incisive remark • **departed:** left, went out

picked up: took

bride: newly-married girl, spouse • **genially:** in a friendly manner

all agog: very curious

wife: married woman • **abroad:** another country

was a general indulgent feeling that Harry – wicked young scapegrace – had had all the luck. Everyone had always felt indulgent towards Harry. Even the owners of windows that had suffered from his indiscriminate use of a catapult had found their indignation dissipated by young Harry's abject expression of regret. He had broken windows, robbed orchards, poached rabbits, and later had run into debt, got entangled with the local tobacconist's daughter – been disentangled and sent off to Africa – and the village as represented by various ageing spinsters had murmured indulgently. 'Ah, well! Wild oats! He'll settle down!'

And now, sure enough, the prodigal had returned – not in affliction, but in triumph. Harry Laxton had 'made good' as the saying goes. He had pulled himself together, worked hard, and had finally met and successfully wooed a young Anglo-French girl who was the possessor of a considerable fortune.

Harry might have lived in London, or purchased an estate in some fashionable hunting county, but he preferred to come back to the part of the world that was home to him. And there, in the most romantic way, he purchased the derelict estate in the dower house of which he had passed his childhood.

Kingsdean House had been unoccupied for nearly seventy years. It had gradually fallen into decay and abandon. An elderly caretaker and his wife lived in the one habitable corner of it. It was a vast, unprepossessing grandiose mansion, the gardens overgrown with rank vegetation and the trees hemming it in like some gloomy enchanter's den.

The dower house was a pleasant, unpretentious house and had been let for a long term of years to Major Laxton, Harry's father. As a boy, Harry had roamed over the Kingsdean estate and knew every inch of the tangled woods, and the old house itself had always fascinated him.

Major Laxton had died some years ago, so it might have been thought that Harry would have had no ties to bring him back – nevertheless it was to the home of his boyhood that Harry brought his bride. The ruined old Kingsdean House was pulled down. An army of builders and contractors swooped

feeling: *sentiment* • **wicked:** morally bad
scapegrace: villain, unscrupulous man • **luck:** good fortune
towards: for • **even:** and also • **owners:** proprietors
indiscriminate: disorderly
abject: servile
robbed: pillaged • **orchards:** gardens with fruit trees
poached: illegally taken • **run into:** contracted • **got entangled:** became involved, trapped • **disentangled:** liberated ≠ entangled
off: away, far • **as:** as it was
ageing: (growing) old • **spinsters:** unmarried women • **wild oats:** juvenile conduct! • **settle down:** become calmer, more reasonable
sure enough: confirming their expectations
made good: been successful
saying: proverb • **goes:** expresses it • **pulled himself together:** abandoned his dissipation • **met:** encountered • **wooed:** tried to gain the love of

might: possibility • **purchased:** acquired • **estate:** property
fashionable: chic • **hunting county:** place where you can chase animals (foxes, etc) • **world:** universe • **home to him:** his native land • **most:** extremely, very • **derelict:** in poor condition
dower house: inherited family house • **of which:** situated in the estate and where • **for:** during • **nearly:** approximately
into: indicates transformation • **decay:** ruin
elderly: old • **caretaker:** man in charge of the house
corner: place • **unprepossessing:** unattractive, unpleasant
mansion: manor • **overgrown:** all covered • **rank:** dense like a jungle • **hemming:** bordering • **gloomy:** sinister • **den:** cavern

let: used in return for money • **term of years:** period, time
as: when he was • **roamed over:** walked everywhere in
every inch: the entire surface • **tangled woods:** confused mass of trees
some: a certain number • **ago:** before • **it might ... thought:** people could possibly have thought • **ties:** attachment
nevertheless: in spite of that • **his boyhood:** the period when he was a boy, a child • **brought:** took, came with
pulled down: destroyed • **contractors:** *entrepreneurs*

down upon the place, and in almost a miraculously short space of time – so marvellously does wealth tell – the new house rose white and gleaming among the trees.

Next came a posse of gardeners and after them a procession of furniture vans.

The house was ready. Servants arrived. Lastly, a costly limousine deposited Harry and Mrs Harry at the front door.

The village rushed to call, and Mrs Price, who owned the largest house, and who considered herself to lead society in the place, sent out cards of invitation for a party 'to meet the bride'.

It was a great event. Several ladies had new frocks for the occasion. Everyone was excited, curious, anxious to see this fabulous creature. They said it was all so like a fairy story!

Miss Harmon, weather-beaten, hearty spinster, threw out her question as she squeezed her way through the crowded drawing-room door. Little Miss Brent, a thin, acidulated spinster, fluttered out information.

'Oh, my dear, quite charming. Such pretty manners. And quite young. Really, you know, it makes one feel quite envious to see someone who has everything like that. Good looks and money and breeding – most distinguished, nothing in the least common about her – and dear Harry so devoted!'

'Ah,' said Miss Harmon, 'it's early days yet!'

Miss Brent's thin nose quivered appreciatively. 'Oh, my dear, do you really think –'

'We all know what Harry is,' said Miss Harmon.

'We know what he was! But I expect now –'

'Ah,' said Miss Harmon, 'men are always the same. Once a gay deceiver, always a gay deceiver. I know them.'

'Dear, dear. Poor young thing.' Miss Brent looked much happier. 'Yes, I expect she'll have trouble with him. Someone ought really to warn her. I wonder if she's heard anything of the old story?

'It seems so very unfair,' said Miss Brent, 'that she should know nothing. So awkward. Especially with only the one chemist's shop in the village.'

down upon (swooped): precipitated themselves on, rushed over
so ... tell: (emphatic) wealth (money) tells (counts) so miraculously
rose: was elevated • **gleaming:** rutilant • **among:** in the middle of
next: after that • **posse:** (informal) troop, group
furniture: tables, chairs, etc. • **vans:** transport vehicles
ready: well-prepared • **lastly:** finally • **costly:** of great value

call: make a visit • **owned:** possessed
largest: biggest • **lead:** act as a leader • **society:** high society
sent out: distributed

event: important day • **several:** a certain number • **frocks:** dresses, costumes for women • **anxious:** very desirous
it was all: everything was • **so like:** very similar to • **fairy:** magical
weather-beaten: tanned by wind and sun • **hearty:** cordial, friendly
squeezed ... through: managed to find a passage among the people at the door • **thin** ≠ corpulent
fluttered out ...: gave information in a state of high excitement
such pretty: so delicate
quite: extremely • **one:** you, people in general
good looks: pleasant facial appearance
breeding: good manners • **nothing in the least:** not at all
devoted: attentive, affectionate
early days yet: it is only the beginning of their married life
quivered: trembled, palpitated

expect: suppose, imagine
are ... the same: never change; same as
deceiver: dissimulator, man telling false things
thing: creature • **looked:** appeared
happier: comp. of happy • **trouble:** problems, difficulty
warn: inform • **wonder:** ask myself • **if she's heard ... of:** if someone has told her
so very: double emphasis • **unfair:** unjust • **should:** subjunctive after "that" • **so awkward:** such a delicate situation • **the one:** this particular • **chemist's shop:** pharmacy

For the erstwhile tobacconist's daughter was now married to Mr Edge, the chemist.

'It would be so much nicer,' said Miss Brent, 'if Mrs Laxton were to deal with Boots in Much Benham.'

'I dare say,' said Miss Harmon, 'that Harry Laxton will suggest that himself.'

And again a significant look passed between them.

'But I certainly think,' said Miss Harmon, 'that she ought to know.'

*

'Beasts!' said Clarice Vane indignantly to her uncle, Doctor Haydock. 'Absolute beasts some people are.'

He looked at her curiously.

She was a tall, dark girl, handsome, warm-hearted and impulsive. Her big brown eyes were alight now with indignation as she said, 'All these cats – saying things – hinting things.'

'About Harry Laxton?'

'Yes, about his affair with the tobacconist's daughter.'

'Oh, that!' The doctor shrugged his shoulders. 'A great many young men have affairs of that kind.'

'Of course they do. And it's all over. So why harp on it? And bring it up years after? It's like ghouls feasting on dead bodies.'

'I dare say, my dear, it does seem like that to you. But you see, they have very little to talk about down here, and so I'm afraid they do tend to dwell upon past scandals. But I'm curious to know why it upsets you so much?'

Clarice Vane bit her lip and flushed. She said, in a curiously muffled voice. 'They – they look so happy. The Laxtons, I mean. They're young and in love, and it's all so lovely for them. I hate to think of it being spoiled by whispers and hints and innuendoes and general beastliness.'

'H'm. I see.'

Clarice went on. 'He was talking to me just now. He's so happy and eager and excited and – yes, thrilled – at having

for: because • **erstwhile:** of the past, mentioned before
chemist: pharmacist
so: emphasizes much • **nicer:** preferable, better • **if ... were to:** was going to • **deal with:** shop at • **Boots:** branch of a famous company of pharmacies • **dare say:** suppose

again: once more, another time
ought to: moral obligation

beasts: brutes, cruel creatures
absolute ... are: emphatic inversion

tall ≠ small • **dark** ≠ blond • **handsome:** beautiful • **warm-hearted:** benevolent, charitable • **alight:** brilliant, shining
these cats: these women! • **hinting:** suggesting

about: concerning • **affair:** love affair
shrugged his shoulders: moved the top part of his back to express indifference • **many:** number of • **kind:** sort
do: have affairs • **over:** finished • **harp:** insist persistently
bring it up: evoke it again • **ghouls:** vampires • **feasting on:** enjoying eating • **bodies:** cadavers

does seem: seems (emphatic)
very little ... about: no subject of conversation • **down here:** in the village • **do tend:** are inclined • **dwell upon:** speak continuously of
upsets: annoys, troubles
bit her lip: expressed pain • **flushed:** blushed
muffled: low, indistinct
mean: indicate (she explains "they") • **lovely:** charming
hate: detest • **spoiled:** damaged • **whispers:** rumours
innuendoes: insinuations • **beastliness:** cruelty

went on: continued • **he:** Harry • **just now:** a moment before
eager: passionate • **excited:** enthusiastic • **thrilled:** very happy

got his heart's desire and rebuilt Kingsdean. He's like a child about it all. And she – well, I don't suppose anything has ever gone wrong in her whole life. She's always had everything. You've seen her. What did you think of her?'

The doctor did not answer at once. For other people, Louise Laxton might be an object of envy. A spoiled darling of fortune. To him she had brought only the refrain of a popular song heard many years ago, *Poor little rich girl –*

A small, delicate figure, with flaxen hair curled rather stiffly round her face and big, wistful blue eyes.

Louise was drooping a little. The long stream of congratulations had tired her. She was hoping it might soon be time to go. Perhaps, even now, Harry might say so. She looked at him sideways. So tall and broad-shouldered with his eager pleasure in this horrible, dull party.

Poor little rich girl –

'Ooph!' It was a sigh of relief.

Harry turned to look at his wife amusedly. They were driving away from the party.

She said, 'Darling, what a frightful party!'

Harry laughed. 'Yes, pretty terrible. Never mind, my sweet. It had to be done, you know. All these old pussies knew me when I lived here as a boy. They'd have been terribly disappointed not to have got a look at you close up.'

Louise made a grimace. She said, 'Shall we have to see a lot of them?'

'What? Oh, no. They'll come and make ceremonious calls with card cases, and you'll return the calls and then you needn't bother any more. You can have your own friends down or whatever you like.'

Louise said, after a minute or two, 'Isn't there anyone amusing living down here?'

'Oh, yes. There's the County, you know. Though you may find them a bit dull, too. Mostly interested in bulbs and dogs and horses. You'll ride, of course. You'll enjoy that. There's a horse over at Eglinton I'd like you to see. A beautiful animal, perfectly trained, no vice in him but plenty of spirit.'

his heart's desire: his love, Louise • **rebuilt:** reconstructed
about it all: with all this • **don't ... anything:** suppose nothing • **ever:** (not) at any time • **gone wrong:** been bad, undesirable

at once: immediately
might be: was probably • **spoiled darling:** excessively loved child, permitted to do all that she wanted • **brought:** evoked, suggested
many years ago: a long time before
figure: appearance • **flaxen:** pale yellow • **curled rather stiffly:** undulated in a severe 1930 style • **wistful:** pensive, nostalgic
drooping: showing her lassitude • **stream:** series, succession
tired: fatigued • **hoping:** desiring • **soon:** before long, quickly
even: just • **might:** could perhaps • **say so:** decide
sideways: indirectly • **broad-shouldered:** with a large back
dull: monotonous

sigh: exhalation • **relief:** deliverance

driving away: going away, departing in their car
frightful: unpleasant, horrible
pretty: absolutely • **never mind:** don't be upset
sweet: darling • **had to be done:** was an obligation • **pussies:** cats
they'd: they would
disappointed: frustrated • **close up:** very near, face to face
shall we have to: are we supposed to
a lot of: a great number of, many
come and make: notice *and*, not *to* between two verbs
calls: visits • **card-cases:** packets, gifts • **return the calls:** visit them
you needn't bother any more: no problem in the future • **have ... down:** invite (from London) • **whatever:** anything, all

living: residing • **down here:** in the village
County: important people of the district • **though:** but
a bit dull: a little insipid • **mostly:** above all • **bulbs:** plants
ride: mount a horse • **enjoy:** take pleasure in, like
over: at a short distance • **I'd like ... see:** I would be pleased if you saw him • **trained:** prepared, exercised • **spirit:** energy

The car slowed down to take the turn into the gates of Kingsdean. Harry wrenched the wheel and swore as a grotesque figure sprang up in the middle of the road and he only just managed to avoid it. It stood there, shaking a fist and shouting after them.

Louise clutched his arm. 'Who's that – that horrible old woman?'

Harry's brow was black. 'That's old Murgatroyd. She and her husband were caretakers in the old house. They were there for nearly thirty years.'

'Why does she shake her fist at you?'

Harry's face got red. 'She – well, she resented the house being pulled down. And she got the sack, of course. Her husband's been dead two years. They say she got a bit queer after he died.'

'Is she – she isn't – starving?'

Louise's ideas were vague and somewhat melodramatic. Riches prevented you coming into contact with reality.

Harry was outraged. 'Good Lord, Louise, what an idea! I pensioned her off, of course – and handsomely, too! Found her a new cottage and everything.'

Louise asked, bewildered, 'Then why does she mind?'

Harry was frowning, his brows drawn together. 'Oh, how should I know? Craziness! She loved the house.'

'But it was a ruin, wasn't it?'

'Of course it was – crumbling to pieces – roof leaking – more or less unsafe. All the same I suppose it meant something to her. She'd been there a long time. Oh, I don't know! The old devil's cracked, I think.'

Louise said uneasily, 'She – I think she cursed us. Oh, Harry, I wish she hadn't.'

It seemed to Louise that her new home was tainted and poisoned by the malevolent figure of one crazy old woman. When she went out in the car, when she rode, when she walked out with the dogs, there was always the same figure waiting. Crouched down on herself, a battered hat over wisps of iron-grey hair, and the slow muttering of imprecations.

slowed down: reduced speed • **gates:** portal (entrance)
wrenched the wheel: changed direction violently • **swore:** used blasphemous language • **sprang up:** appeared suddenly
managed to: succeeded in • **to avoid:** not to touch • **shaking a fist:** agitating a closed hand • **shouting after:** insulting loudly
clutched: seized firmly

his brow was black: his face expressed anger, displeasure
husband: married man • **caretakers:** keepers, wardens
for: during • **nearly:** more or less

got: became • **resented:** felt the injustice of
pulled down: demolished • **got the sack:** was turned out of the house, evicted • **two years:** for two years • **a bit queer:** a little strange, not quite there • **died:** ceased to live, departed
starving: having nothing to eat, suffering from hunger
somewhat: a little
riches: fortune • **prevented:** stopped, made unable (to come)
outraged: angry, furious
pensioned ... off: paid a pension when she left • **handsomely:** generously • **found:** offered
bewildered: perplexed • **mind:** resent, protest
frowning: expressing discontent • **brows:** hairs over the eyes • **how should I know:** impossible to know • **craziness:** madness, insanity
wasn't it: asking for confirmation
crumbling to pieces: deteriorating • **roof:** housetop • **leaking** ≠ water-proof • **unsafe:** dangerous • **meant:** represented
long time: nearly thirty years
devil: creature • **cracked:** crazy, deranged
uneasily: perturbed, not at ease • **cursed:** sent maledictions on
hadn't: hadn't cursed

tainted: polluted
malevolent: malefic • **figure:** presence
went out ... car: took the car for a drive
waiting: standing there, not moving
crouched down: bent • **battered:** decrepit • **wisps ... hair:** rare, thin hair • **muttering:** incomprehensible expression

Louise came to believe that Harry was right – the old woman was mad. Nevertheless that did not make things easier. Mrs Murgatroyd never actually came to the house, nor did she use definite threats, nor offer violence. Her squatting figure remained always just outside the gates. To appeal to the police would have been useless and, in any case, Harry Laxton was averse to that course of action. It would, he said, arouse local sympathy for the old brute. He took the matter more easily than Louise did.

'Don't worry about it, darling. She'll get tired of this silly cursing business. Probably she's only trying it on.'

'She isn't, Harry. She – she hates us! I can feel it. She – she's ill-wishing us.'

'She's not a witch, darling, although she may look like one! Don't be morbid about it all.'

Louise was silent. Now that the first excitement of settling in was over, she felt curiously lonely and at a loose end. She had been used to life in London and the Riviera. She had no knowledge of or taste for English country life. She was ignorant of gardening, except for the final act of 'doing the flowers'. She did not really care for dogs. She was bored by such neighbours as she met. She enjoyed riding best, sometimes with Harry, sometimes, when he was busy about the estate, by herself. She hacked through the woods and lanes, enjoying the easy paces of the beautiful horse that Harry had bought for her. Yet even Prince Hal, most sensitive of chestnut steeds, was wont to shy and snort as he carried his mistress past the huddled figure of a malevolent old woman.

One day Louise took her courage in both hands. She was out walking. She had passed Mrs Murgatroyd, pretending not to notice her, but suddenly she swerved back and went right up to her. She said, a little breathlessly, 'What is it? What's the matter? What do you want?'

The old woman blinked at her. She had a cunning, dark gypsy face, with wisps of iron-grey hair, and bleared, suspicious eyes. Louise wondered if she drank.

She spoke in a whining and yet threatening voice. 'What do I want, you ask? What, indeed! That which has been took

came to believe: finally thought • **was right:** what he said corresponded to reality • **nevertheless:** however • **did not ... easier:** facilitate the situation • **actually:** really • **never... nor did:** note inversion with negation • **threats:** menaces
remained: did not move from her place • **outside:** on the other side of • **useless:** vain • **in any case:** anyway, in all circumstances
averse: opposed
arouse: raise, provoke • **took the matter:** accepted the situation
easily: quietly, calmly
worry: be alarmed • **silly:** stupid, absurd, idiotic
trying it on: testing our patience

ill-wishing us: desiring bad, horrible things for us
witch: sorceress • **although:** in spite of the fact that
one (look like): resemble a witch
settling in: moving in, taking possession of her home
lonely: solitary, alone • **at a loose end:** having nothing specific to do • **used:** accustomed • **had no knowledge:** knew nothing
taste: interest • **country:** rural
doing the flowers: assembling bouquets
care for: love • **bored:** not interested
such neighbours as: the sort of people in the vicinity that
busy about: occupied with
by herself: without company • **hacked:** rode slowly • **woods and lanes:** trees and small roads
most ... of: more ... than all the others • **chestnut:** *alezan*
steeds: riding-horses • **wont:** accustomed • **shy and snort:** turn away brusquely and make a sound with its nose • **past:** in front of
huddled figure: confused mass
passed: gone past
swerved back: returned abruptly • **right up to:** exactly in front of, face to face • **breathlessly:** with quick respiration
matter: problem
blinked: shut and opened her eyes quickly • **cunning:** perfidious
bleared: filmy, half-blind
wondered: asked herself • **drank:** drank alcohol
whining: plaintive • **yet:** all the same • **threatening:** emitting threats • **indeed:** really • **that:** the house • **took:** taken

away from me. Who turned me out of Kingsdean House? I'd lived there, girl and woman, for near on forty years. It was a black deed to turn me out and it's black bad luck it'll bring to you and him!'

Louise said, 'You've got a very nice cottage and –'

She broke off. The old woman's arms flew up. She screamed, 'What's the good of that to me? It's my own place I want and my own fire as I sat beside all them years. And as for you and him, I'm telling you there will be no happiness for you in your new fine house. It's the black sorrow will be upon you! Sorrow and death and my curse. May your fair face rot.'

Louise turned away and broke into a little stumbling run. She thought, *I must get away from here! We must sell the house! We must go away.*

At the moment, such a solution seemed easy to her. But Harry's utter incomprehension took her aback. He exclaimed, 'Leave here? Sell the house? Because of a crazy old woman's threats? You must be mad.'

'No, I'm not. But she – she frightens me, I know something will happen.'

Harry Laxton said grimly, 'Leave Mrs Murgatroyd to me. I'll settle her!'

A friendship had sprung up between Clarice Vane and young Mrs Laxton. The two girls were much of an age, though dissimilar both in character and in tastes. In Clarice's company, Louise found reassurance. Clarice was so self-reliant, so sure of herself. Louise mentioned the matter of Mrs Murgatroyd and her threats, but Clarice seemed to regard the matter as more annoying than frightening.

'It's so stupid, that sort of thing,' she said. 'And really very annoying for you.'

'You know, Clarice, I – I feel quite frightened sometimes. My heart gives the most awful jumps.'

'Nonsense, you mustn't let a silly thing like that get you down. She'll soon tire of it.'

... away from me: taken illegally by force • **turned out of:** ejected from • **lived:** resided • **near on:** approximately
black deed: bad action • **bad luck:** sinister augur, presage

you've got: you possess
broke off: stopped speaking brusquely • **the old ... up:** she brandished her arms • **screamed:** cried • **good:** benefit • **own:** emphasis • **as ... beside:** where I was accustomed to sit • **them:** those (note the incorrect language she uses) • **telling:** predicting
fine: beautiful • **black:** note the repetition • **will be:** that will be
sorrow: distress • **death** ≠ life • **curse:** malediction
rot: be decomposed, decay
turned away: changed direction to return • **broke ... run:** began trotting hesitantly • **get away ... here:** quit the place • **sell** ≠ buy
away: far from here (note the repetition of *must*)
the moment: that moment • **easy** ≠ difficult
utter: complete, absolute • **took her aback:** shocked her
crazy: insane, foolish, stupid
you must be mad: you've lost your reason, you are certainly deranged • **frightens:** terrifies • **something ... happen:** something bad will take place
grimly: menacingly • **leave ... to me:** I'll treat with Mrs M. myself
settle: render her inoffensive

friendship: amicable relation • **sprung up:** developed rapidly
much of an age: nearly the same age • **though dissimilar:** in spite of their differences • **both:** at the same time • **tastes:** interests
so: to such a degree • **self-reliant:** independent
mentioned: alluded to • **matter:** problem
regard: consider • **as:** in a certain manner
annoying: irritating

quite : so • **sometimes:** at certain times
the most: superlative of *more* • **awful:** terrible • **jumps:** sudden beatings • **nonsense:** it's absurd • **let:** permit • **get you down:** depress you • **tire of it:** be tired of it, find no interest in it

She was silent for a minute or two. Clarice said, 'What's the matter?'

Louise paused for a minute, then her answer came with a rush. 'I hate this place! I hate being here. The woods and this house, and the awful silence at night, and the queer noise owls make. Oh, and the people and everything.'

'The people. What people?'

'The people in the village. Those prying, gossiping old maids.'

Clarice said sharply, 'What have they been saying?'

'I don't know. Nothing particular. But they've got nasty minds. When you've talked to them you feel you wouldn't trust anybody – not anybody at all.'

Clarice said harshly, 'Forget them. They've nothing to do but gossip. And most of the muck they talk they just invent.'

Louise said, 'I wish we'd never come here. But Harry adores it so.' Her voice softened.

Clarice thought, *How she adores him!* She said abruptly, 'I must go now.'

'I'll send you back in the car. Come again soon.'

Clarice nodded. Louise felt comforted by her new friend's visit. Harry was pleased to find her more cheerful and from then on urged her to have Clarice often to the house.

Then one day he said, 'Good news for you, darling.'

'Oh, what?'

'I've fixed the Murgatroyd. She's got a son in America, you know. Well, I've arranged for her to go out and join him. I'll pay her passage.'

'Oh, Harry, how wonderful! I believe I might get to like Kingsdean after all.'

'Get to like it? Why, it's the most wonderful place in the world!'

Louise gave a little shiver. She could not rid herself of her superstitious fear so easily.

what's the matter?: what's wrong, what's the problem?

paused: continued to be silent • **with a rush:** with precipitation
hate: dislike intensely
night ≠ day • **queer:** bizarre, weird • **noise:** cry, call
owls: nocturnal birds of prey with large eyes and unpleasant cries
people: population, inhabitants
prying: inquisitive • **gossiping:** propagating rumours
maids: spinsters
sharply: incisively • **saying:** telling, revealing
nasty: bad, unpleasant
minds: intentions, ideas
trust: believe, have confidence in • **not anybody:** no one
harshly: brusquely • **forget** ≠ remember, keep in memory
but: except • **most of:** nearly all, the greatest part • **muck:** disgusting rumours, scandals
I wish: if only • **we'd:** we had
so: so much • **softened:** became softer, tender
abruptly: notice Clarice's trenchant way of speaking as if she was not at ease
I'll send ... car: the chauffeur will take you home
nodded: approved with her head • **comforted:** consoled
cheerful: happy and optimistic, joyous • **from then on:** in the future
urged: encouraged, pressed • **to have ... house:** to invite Clarice to come

fixed: made arrangements with • **the Murgatroyd:** pejorative for Mrs M. • **go out and join him:** leave England and go to America
passage: ticket to go there
wonderful: marvellous • **might:** possibility • **get to like:** finally become attached to
why: exclamation of surprise, not a question • **in the world:** note *in* after superlative, not *of*
gave ... shiver: trembled a little • **rid herself of:** liberate herself from • **fear:** terror • **easily:** quickly, not without difficulty

If the ladies of St Mary Mead had hoped for the pleasure of imparting information about her husband's past to the bride, this pleasure was denied them by Harry Laxton's own prompt action.

Miss Harmon and Clarice Vane were both in Mr Edge's shop, the one buying mothballs and the other a packet of boracic, when Harry Laxton and his wife came in.

After greeting the two ladies, Harry turned to the counter and was just demanding a toothbrush when he stopped in mid-speech and exclaimed heartily, 'Well, well, just see who's here! Bella, I do declare.'

Mrs Edge, who had hurried out from the back parlour to attend to the congestion of business, beamed back cheerfully at him, showing her big white teeth. She had been a dark, handsome girl and was still a reasonably handsome woman, though she had put on weight, and the lines of her face had coarsened; but her large brown eyes were full of warmth as she answered, 'Bella, it is, Mr Harry, and pleased to see you after all these years.'

Harry turned to his wife. 'Bella's an old flame of mine, Louise,' he said. 'Head-over-heels in love with her, wasn't I, Bella?'

'That's what you say,' said Mrs Edge.

Louise laughed. She said, 'My husband's very happy seeing all his old friends again.'

'Ah,' said Mrs Edge, 'we haven't forgotten you, Mr Harry. Seems like a fairy tale to think of you married and building up a new house instead of that ruined old Kingsdean House.'

'You look very well and blooming,' said Harry, and Mrs Edge laughed and said there was nothing wrong with her and what about that toothbrush?

Clarice, watching the baffled look on Miss Harmon's face, said to herself exultantly, *Oh, well done, Harry. You've spiked their guns.*

Doctor Haydock said abruptly to his niece, 'What's all this nonsense about old Mrs Murgatroyd hanging about Kingsdean and shaking her fist and cursing the new regime?'

hoped for: anticipated, expected
imparting: communicating • **about:** related to, in connection with
denied: refused to • **own ... action:** the action he did himself

both: the two of them, together
the one ... the other: the first ... the second • **mothballs:** naphthalene • **boracic:** boric acid, sort of antiseptic • **came in:** entered the shop • **greeting:** saluting • **turned to:** faced
toothbrush: dental brush • **stopped ... mid-speech:** didn't finish his request • **heartily:** cheerfully • **well:** exclamation of surprise
I do declare: I announce with emphasis (surprise) **hurried out:** come out in haste • **to attend to:** to serve, to help
the congestion of business: the numerous clients • **beamed ... him:** reciprocated his joy • **showing ... teeth:** smiling with open mouth • **handsome:** attractive • **still:** up to now • **reasonably:** moderately • **though:** but • **put on weight:** become corpulent
coarsened (had): were more apparent • **large:** big • **warmth:** cordiality • **Bella, it is:** yes, I am Bella

B's: B. is • **is an old flame of mine:** I loved her in the past
head-over-heels: passionately • **wasn't I:** asking for confirmation

laughed: expressed hilarity
again: one more time
forgotten: pp of forget ≠ remember (forget, forgot, forgotten)
seems: it seems • **fairy tale:** enchanted story • **building up:** constructing • **instead of:** in the place of
look: appear, seem • **very well:** in good form • **blooming:** fresh
there was nothing wrong: everything was all right, ok
and what about ...: she turns back to the present situation
watching: observing • **baffled:** disconcerted • **look:** expression
exultantly: full of jubilation • **well done:** good work! • **spiked their guns:** frustrated them in their plans

nonsense: ridiculous stories • **hanging:** persistently present • **shaking her fist:** with a menacing hand • **regime:** situation, circumstances

'It isn't nonsense. It's quite true. It's upset Louise a good deal.'

'Tell her she needn't worry – when the Murgatroyds were caretakers they never stopped grumbling about the place – they only stayed because Murgatroyd drank and couldn't get another job.'

'I'll tell her,' said Clarice doubtfully, 'but I don't think she'll believe you. The old woman fairly screams with rage.'

'Always used to be fond of Harry as a boy. I can't understand it.'

Clarice said, 'Oh, well – they'll be rid of her soon. Harry's paying her passage to America.'

Three days later, Louise was thrown from her horse and killed.

Two men in a baker's van were witnesses of the accident. They saw Louise ride out of the gates, saw the old woman spring up and stand in the road waving her arms and shouting, saw the horse start, swerve, and then bolt madly down the road, flinging Louise Laxton over his head.

One of them stood over the unconscious figure, not knowing what to do, while the other rushed to the house to get help.

Harry Laxton came running out, his face ghastly. They took off a door of the van and carried her on it to the house. She died without regaining consciousness and before the doctor arrived.

(End of Doctor Haydock's manuscript.)

When Doctor Haydock arrived the following day, he was pleased to note that there was a pink flush in Miss Marple's cheek and decidedly more animation in her manner.

'Well,' he said, 'what's the verdict?'

'What's the problem, Doctor Haydock?' countered Miss Marple.

'Oh, my dear lady, do I have to tell you that?'

'I suppose,' said Miss Marple, 'that it's the curious conduct of the caretaker. Why did she behave in that very odd way? People do mind being turned out of their old homes. But it wasn't her home. In fact, she used to complain and grumble

true: authentic, real • **upset:** perturbed • **a good deal:** very much

needn't: had no reason to • **worry:** be anxious
grumbling: complaining • **place:** house
stay: did not go away • **drank:** consumed alcohol in excess
get: obtain
doubtfully: uncertain about the result
believe you: think what you say is true • **fairly:** absolutely
used to be fond of: felt affection for in the past • **understand:** perceive the reason for it
rid: liberated, delivered • **soon:** in a short time, promptly

later: after • **was thrown:** was ejected
killed: expired, perished
baker: person making bread • **were witnesses of:** had seen (with their own eyes) • **ride out of the gates:** leave the house on her horse • **waving:** brandishing • **shouting:** screaming
start: move brusquely • **swerve:** change direction • **bolt madly:** run furiously • **flinging ... head:** dislodging L.L. and she fell in front of the horse • **stood over:** stood beside, near • **figure:** body
while: at the same time • **rushed:** ran precipitously
help: aid
ghastly: livid, deathy pale
took off: detached • **carried:** transported

the following day: the day after
pink flush: fresh rosy colour, blush
cheek: face • **decidedly:** undoubtedly • **more animation ... manner:** she had regained dynamism, energy
countered: reacted to his question with another question

do I have to?: is it necessary to? • **tell you that:** explain where the problem is • **curious conduct:** strange manner in which she acted
why: for what reason • **behave:** conduct herself • **odd:** queer
do mind: feel real resentment • **turned out of:** expelled from
grumble: recriminate

while she was there. Yes, it certainly looks very fishy. What became of her, by the way?'

'Did a bunk to Liverpool. The accident scared her. Thought she'd wait there for her boat.'

'All very convenient for somebody,' said Miss Marple. 'Yes, I think the "Problem of the Caretaker's Conduct" can be solved easily enough. Bribery, was it not?'

'That's your solution?'

'Well, if it wasn't natural for her to behave in that way, she must have been "putting on an act" as people say, and that means that somebody paid her to do what she did.'

'And you know who that somebody was?'

'Oh, I think so. Money again, I'm afraid. And I've always noticed that gentlemen always tend to admire the same type.'

'Now I'm out of my depth.'

'No, no, it all hangs together. Harry Laxton admired Bella Edge, a dark, vivacious type. Your niece Clarice was the same. But the poor little wife was quite a different type – fair-haired and clinging – not his type at all. So he must have married her for her money. And murdered her for her money, too!'

'You use the word 'murder'?'

'Well, he sounds the right type. Attractive to women and quite unscrupulous. I suppose he wanted to keep his wife's money and marry your niece. He may have been seen talking to Mrs Edge. But I don't fancy he was attached to her any more. Though I dare say he made the poor woman think he was, for ends of his own. He soon had her well under his thumb, I fancy.'

'How exactly did he murder her, do you think?'

Miss Marple stared ahead of her for some minutes with dreamy blue eyes.

'It was very well timed – with the baker's van as witness. They could see the old woman and, of course, they'd put down the horse's fright to that. But I should imagine, myself, that an air gun, or perhaps a catapult. Yes, just as the horse came through the gates. The horse bolted, of course, and

looks: seems • **fishy:** dishonest, ambiguous • **what became of her:** what happened to her • **by the way:** in passing
did a bunk: escaped furtively • **scared:** frightened
wait: stay • **for her boat:** for her departure to America
all: all that • **convenient:** opportune, favorable

solved: explained • **easily:** without effort • **bribery:** corruption

behave: comport herself • **in that way:** like that
must have been: probability in the past • **putting on an act:** playing a role • **means:** signifies

think so: believe I know • **I'm afraid:** I regret to say
always: at all times • **tend:** are inclined to
I'm out of my depth: I'm unable to understand, it's too difficult for me
hangs together: makes sense, is coherent
dark ≠ blond • **vivacious:** cheerful and energetic
quite: completely, absolutely
fair-haired: blond • **clinging:** dependent (on him) • **so:** consequently
murdered: killed
too: in addition, moreover

sounds: gives the impresion to be • **right:** exact, precise
unscrupulous: having no moral principles • **keep:** retain possession • **may have been:** supposition in the past
fancy: imagine, believe • **any more:** any longer (he had ceased to love her) • **though:** but • **dare say:** suppose • **poor:** pitiful
was: was attached to her • **ends ... own:** personal motives • **well under his thumb:** under his complete control, influence

stared ahead of her: looked intently in front of her
dreamy: pensive
timed: synchronized • **as:** for
of course: naturally • **put down:** attributed
to that: to the sudden appearance of the woman
that: that there were other causes, a compressed-air rifle, etc.
bolted: galloped furiously

Mrs Laxton was thrown.'

She paused, frowning.

'The fall might have killed her. But he couldn't be sure of that. And he seems the sort of man who would lay his plans carefully and leave nothing to chance. After all, Mrs Edge could get him something suitable without her husband knowing. Otherwise, why would Harry bother with her? Yes, I think he had some powerful drug handy, that could be administered before you arrived. After all, if a woman is thrown from her horse and has serious injuries and dies without recovering consciousness, well – a doctor wouldn't normally be suspicious, would he? He'd put it down to shock or something.'

Doctor Haydock nodded.

'Why did you suspect?' asked Miss Marple.

'It wasn't any particular cleverness on my part,' said Doctor Haydock. 'It was just the trite, well-known fact that a murderer is so pleased with his cleverness that he doesn't take proper precautions. I was just saying a few consolatory words to the bereaved husband – and feeling damned sorry for the fellow, too – when he flung himself down on the settee to do a bit of play-acting and a hypodermic syringe fell out of his pocket.

'He snatched it up and looked so scared that I began to think. Harry Laxton didn't drug; he was in perfect health; what was he doing with a hypodermic syringe? I did the autopsy with a view to certain possibilities. I found strophanthin. The rest was easy. There was strophanthin in Laxton's possession, and Bella Edge, questioned by the police, broke down and admitted to having got it for him. And finally old Mrs Murgatroyd confessed that it was Harry Laxton who had put her up to the cursing stunt.'

'And your niece got over it?'

'Yes, she was attracted by the fellow, but it hadn't gone far.'

The doctor picked up his manuscript.

'Full marks to you, Miss Marple – and full marks to me for my prescription. You're looking almost yourself again.'

was thrown: fell down (fall, fell, fallen)
paused: stopped talking • **frowning:** expressing perplexity
might have: had possibly • **he:** Mr Laxton
lay his plans: prepare his actions, decide
carefully: with great attention, care • **chance:** hazard
get him: obtain for him • **suitable:** appropriate • **without ... knowing:** secretly • **otherwise:** if not • **bother with:** be concerned with • **powerful:** efficacious • **handy:** near-at-hand, ready to be used
serious injuries: severe physical pains
recovering: regaining
be suspicious: suspect anything • **would he:** asking for approbation • **something:** something like that
nodded: acquiesced

cleverness: subtlety • **on my part:** from me
trite: common, banal • **well-known:** known by everybody
pleased with: satisfied with
proper: adequate • **just:** only • **a few:** some
bereaved: solitary, abandoned • **damned sorry:** extremely sad, full of compassion • **flung ... settee:** let himself fall on the sofa • **do ... acting:** play a role like an actor • **syringe:** used to inoculate some drug
snatched it up: seized it back quickly • **scared:** terrified
think: (that there was something fishy) • **drug:** take drugs himself

with a view to: having in mind, thinking of • **strophanthin:** a poisonous substance used as heart stimulant
broke down: cracked up, lost his self-control
admitted to having: admitted she had

put her up to: urged, pressed her to • **cursing stunt:** theatrical malediction scenes • **got over it:** surmounted it, recovered from it
it hadn't gone far: the affair hadn't taken much importance

picked up: seized, took hold of
full marks: complete success, 20 out of 20 !
you're ... again: you have regained your form, it seems

Magnolia Blossom

I

Vincent Easton was waiting under the clock at Victoria Station. Now and then he glanced up at it uneasily. He thought to himself: 'How many other men have waited here for a woman who didn't come?'

A sharp pang shot through him. Supposing that Theo didn't come, that she had changed her mind? Women did that sort of thing. Was he sure of her – had he ever been sure of her? Did he really know anything at all about her? Hadn't she puzzled him from the first? There had seemed to be two women – the lovely, laughing creature who was Richard Darell's wife, and the other – silent, mysterious, who had walked by his side in the garden of Haymer's Close. Like a magnolia flower – that was how he thought of her – perhaps because it was under the magnolia tree that they had tasted their first rapturous, incredulous kiss. The air had been sweet with the scent of magnolia bloom, and one or two petals, velvety-soft and fragrant, had floated down, resting on that upturned face that was as creamy and as soft and as silent as they. Magnolia blossom – exotic, fragrant, mysterious.

That had been a fortnight ago – the second day he had met her. And now he was waiting for her to come to him forever. Again incredulity shot through him. She wouldn't come. How could he ever have believed it? It would be giving up so much. The beautiful Mrs Darrell couldn't do this sort of thing quietly. It was bound to be a nine days' wonder, a far-reaching scandal that would never quite be forgotten. There were better, more expedient ways of doing these things – a discreet divorce, for instance.

But they had never thought of that for a moment – at least he had not. Had she, he wondered? He had never known anything of her thoughts. He had asked her to come away with him almost timorously – for after all, what was he?

waiting: standing • **Victoria Station:** railway station
now and then: from time to time • **glanced:** looked briefly • **thought to himself:** meditated • **how many:** what number

sharp: intense • **pang:** sudden suffering • **shot ... him:** pierced his heart • **mind:** intention, decision • **did ... thing:** had a tendency to be changeable • **had he ... been:** pluperfect expressing action in the past with effects in the present • **about her:** concerning her • **puzzled him:** made him perplexed • **the first:** the beginning • **lovely:** beautiful • **laughing:** gay, joyous
Darell's wife: married to R. Darell
walked: had a promenade • **by his side:** with him • **close:** enclosed property (of a church) • **how:** in that manner
under: at the base of • **tasted:** savoured
rapturous: delicious • **incredulous:** incredible • **sweet:** pleasantly perfumed • **scent:** odour • **bloom:** flowers
velvety-soft: delicate like velvet • **fragrant:** odoriferous
upturned: horizontal (she looked up at him) • **as they:** as they were

a fortnight ago: two weeks before

forever: in perpetuity
ever: at one moment • **believed it:** thought it possible • **giving up:** renunciation of • **so much:** a great quantity of things
quietly: discreetly • **bound ... wonder:** inevitably a scandal • **far-reaching:** with considerable consequences • **forgotten:** effaced from memory • **ways:** methods
for instance: for example
thought of that: envisaged that possibility • **at least:** in any case
wondered: reflected • **never known ... thoughts:** never discovered her state of mind • **come away:** quit her husband and go with him • **timorously:** with timidity

Nobody in particular – one of a thousand orange growers in the Transvaal. What a life to take her to – after the brilliance of London! And yet, since he wanted her so desperately, he must needs ask.

She had consented very quietly, with no hesitations or protests, as though it were the simplest thing in the world that he was asking her.

'Tomorrow?' he had said, amazed, almost unbelieving.

And she had promised in that soft, broken voice that was so different from the laughing brilliance of her social manner. He had compared her to a diamond when he first saw her – a thing of flashing fire, reflecting light from a hundred facets. But at that first touch, that first kiss, she had changed miraculously to the clouded softness of a pearl – a pearl like a magnolia blossom, creamy-pink.

She had promised. And now he was waiting for her to fulfil that promise.

He looked again at the clock. If she did not come soon, they would miss the train.

Sharply a wave of reaction set in. She wouldn't come! Of course she wouldn't come. Fool that he had been ever to expect it! What were promises? He would find a letter when he got back to his rooms – explaining, protesting, saying all the things that women do when they are excusing themselves for lack of courage.

He felt anger – anger and the bitterness of frustration.

Then he saw her coming towards him down the platform, a faint smile on her face. She walked slowly, without haste or fluster, as one who had all eternity before her. She was in black – soft black that clung, with a little black hat that framed the wonderful creamy pallor of her face.

He found himself grasping her hand, muttering stupidly:

'So you've come – you have come. After all!'

'Of course.'

How calm her voice sounded! How calm!

'I thought you wouldn't,' he said, releasing her hand and breathing hard.

nobody in particular: not a special person • **growers:** planters
Transvaal: part of South Africa • **take her to:** transport her to a new life • **yet:** in spite of that • **wanted:** desired to possess
must needs: must absolutely
quietly: calmly
as though: as if; note *were* subj., but *was* is common in modern English
amazed: stupefied • **unbelieving:** incredulous
broken: halting
laughing brilliance: gay vivacity • **her social manner:** the tone of voice she used in society • **first:** for the first time
a thing of: something like • **flashing fire:** brilliant flames
touch: contact • **changed ... to:** been transformed into
clouded: opaque • **softness:** delicate texture

for her to: until she; note infinitive form
fulfil: execute, accomplish
soon: in a short time
miss the train: the train will be gone
sharply: abruptly • **a wave ... set in:** he was invaded by a violent reaction • **fool:** stupid, ridiculous
expect it: suppose she would come • **find:** receive, discover
got back: returned • **rooms:** apartment
do: say
lack: absence
anger: rage • **bitterness:** virulence
coming towards ... platform: walking in his direction from the end of the train • **faint:** vague • **smile:** expression of pleasure
fluster: agitation
soft black: supple black costume • **clung:** showed the forms of her body, fitted her • **framed:** encircled
found ... hand: seized her hand automatically • **muttering:** murmured inaudibly
of course: naturally
sounded: gave the impression (ob being calm)
you wouldn't: you would not come • **releasing:** disengaging
breathing hard: inhaling and exhaling more than normal

Her eyes opened – wide, beautiful eyes. There was wonder in them, the simple wonder of a child.

'Why?'

He didn't answer. Instead he turned aside and requisitioned a passing porter. They had not much time. The next few minutes were all bustle and confusion. Then they were sitting in their reserved compartment and the drab houses of southern London were drifting by them.

II

Theodora Darrell was sitting opposite him. At last she was his. And he knew now how incredulous, up to the very last minute, he had been. He had not dared to let himself believe. That magical, elusive quality about her had frightened him. It had seemed impossible that she should ever belong to him.

Now the suspense was over. The irrevocable step was taken. He looked across at her. She lay back in the corner, quite still. The faint smile lingered on her lips, her eyes were cast down, the long, black lashes swept the creamy curve of her cheek.

He thought: 'What's in her mind now? What is she thinking of? Me? Her husband? What does she think about him anyway? Did she care for him once? Or did she never care? Does she hate him, or is she indifferent to him?' And with a pang the thought swept through him: 'I don't know. I never shall know. I love her, and I don't know anything about her – what she thinks or what she feels.'

His mind circled round the thought of Theodora Darrell's husband. He had known plenty of married women who were only too ready to talk about their husbands – of how they were misunderstood by them, of how their finer feelings were ignored. Vincent Easton reflected cynically that it was one of the best-known opening gambits.

But except casually, Theo had never spoken of Richard Darrell. Easton knew of him what everybody knew. He was a popular man, handsome, with an engaging, carefree manner.

opened: expressed surprise • **wide:** large • **wonder:** an expression of incredulity
why?: for what reason?
instead: in place of answering • **requisitioned:** demanded the service of • **porter:** person employed to carry baggage • **next:** coming • **bustle:** agitation • **confusion:** disorder • **then:** finally
drab: monotonous
drifting by: passing slowly in front of them

opposite: facing
his: his property • **up to ... minute:** just before this moment
dared: had the courage • **let himself believe:** admit that it was real
elusive: impalpable • **about:** in • **frightened:** terrified
should: probability • **ever:** one day • **belong to him:** be his
suspense: uncertainty • **over:** finished • **step:** decision
across: on the opposite side • **lay back:** sat comfortably
quite: completely • **still:** immobile • **lingered:** persisted
cast down: closed • **lashes:** eyelashes • **swept:** caressed
cheek: part of the face under the eye
what's in...now: what ideas is she having • **is she thinking of:** the object of her reflection (thing *of* sth)
anyway: in any case • **care:** feel affection • **once:** in the past
hate: detest
pang: piercing pain • **swept through:** invaded him
I never shall know: I'll never know (the future *I shall* was considered more correct than *I will*)
circled round: turned round and round • **thought:** subject
plenty of: a great amount of
ready: prompt, willing
misunderstood: suffered from incomprehension • **finer feelings:** more delicate emotions
opening gambit: stratagem, tactics
casually: incidentally • **spoken of:** mentioned
popular: appreciated • **handsome:** attractive • **engaging, carefree manner:** open, relaxed attitude

Everybody liked Darrell. His wife always seemed on excellent terms with him. But that proved nothing, Vincent reflected. Theo was well-bred – she would not air her grievances in public.

And between them, no word had passed. From that second evening of their meeting, when they had walked together in the garden, silent, their shoulders touching, and he had felt the faint tremor that shook her at his touch, there had been no explainings, no defining of the position. She had returned his kisses, a dumb, trembling creature, shorn of all that hard brilliance which, together with her cream-and-rose beauty, had made her famous. Never once had she spoken of her husband. Vincent had been thankful for that at the time. He had been glad to be spared the arguments of a woman who wished to assure herself and her lover that they were justified in yielding to their love.

Yet now the tacit conspiracy of silence worried him. He had again that panic-stricken sense of knowing nothing about this strange creature who was willingly linking her life to his. He was afraid.

In the impulse to reassure himself, he bent forward and laid a hand on the black-clad knee opposite him. He felt once again the faint tremor that shook her, and he reached up for her hand. Bending forward, he kissed the palm, a long, lingering kiss. He felt the response of her fingers on his and, looking up, met her eyes, and was content.

He leaned back in his seat. For the moment, he wanted no more. They were together. She was his. And presently he said in a light, almost bantering tone:

'You're very silent?'

'Am I?'

'Yes.' He waited a minute, then said in a graver tone: 'You're sure you don't – regret?'

Her eyes opened wide at that. 'Oh, no!'

He did not doubt the reply. There was an assurance of sincerity behind it.

'What are you thinking about? I want to know.'

In a low voice she answered: 'I think I'm afraid.'

always: at all times; note the place of the adverb before the verb

well-bred: had good manners • **air:** express • **grievances:** reproaches
between them: reciprocally • **no word had passed:** not a word had been pronounced • **evening:** end of day
shoulders touching: close together • **felt:** perceived
faint: imperceptible • **tremor:** trembling • **shook:** agitated
explainings: explanations • **defining:** definition • **returned:** reciprocated • **dumb:** silent • **shorn of:** without • **hard:** cruel
together with: added to, plus
famous: remarkable
been thankful: felt gratitude • **at the time:** at that moment
glad: pleased • **be spared:** not be exposed to
wished: desired
yielding: submitting
yet: but, however • **worried:** troubled
panic-stricken sense: sensation accompanied by panic
willingly: voluntarily • **linking:** uniting

impulse: impulsion • **bent forward:** inclining his body in her direction • **laid a hand:** put his hand • **black-clad:** covered with black material • **reached up for:** raised his hand to seize

lingering: prolonged • **response:** reaction • **his:** his fingers
met his eyes: saw that she was also looking at him • **content:** satisfied • **leaned back:** regained his first position
presently: soon, almost immediately
light ≠ grave • **bantering:** humorous

am I?: really?
he waited a minute: note Vincent's anxiety, his doubts, his hesitations compared to Theodora's calm determination
opened wide: dilated • **that:** that question
assurance of sincerity: convincing sincerity
behind it: suggested in the tone of her voice

low voice: murmur, whisper; ≠ in a loud voice

'Afraid?'

'Of happiness.'

He moved over beside her then, held her to him and kissed the softness of her face and neck.

'I love you,' he said. 'I love you – love you.'

Her answer was in the clinging of her body, the abandon of her lips.

Then he moved back to his own corner. He picked up a magazine and so did she. Every now and then, over the top of the magazines, their eyes met. Then they smiled.

They arrived at Dover just after five. They were to spend the night there, and cross to the Continent on the following day. Theo entered their sitting room in the hotel with Vincent close behind her. He had a couple of evening papers in his hand which he threw down on the table. Two of the hotel servants brought in the luggage and withdrew.

Theo turned from the window where she had been standing looking out. In another minute they were in each other's arms.

There was a discreet tap on the door and they drew apart again.

'Damn it all,' said Vincent, 'it doesn't seem as though we were ever going to be alone.'

Theo smiled. 'It doesn't look like it,' she said softly. Sitting down on the sofa, she picked up one of the papers.

The knock proved to be a waiter bearing tea. He laid it on the table, drawing the latter up to the sofa on which Theo was sitting, cast a deft glance round, inquired if there were anything further, and withdrew.

Vincent, who had gone into the adjoining room, came back into the sitting room.

'Now for tea,' he said cheerily, but stopped suddenly in the middle of the room. 'Anything wrong?' he asked.

Theo was sitting bolt upright on the sofa. She was staring in front of her with dazed eyes, and her face had gone deathly white.

Vincent took a quick step towards her.

'What is it, sweetheart?'

afraid: frightened
happiness: felicity
moved over beside her: came by her side and sat down • **held her up to him:** took her in his arms

clinging: movement of her body attracted to his

moved back: returned • **picked up:** took
so did she: she did the same • **over the top:** glancing up
their eyes met: they looked at each other
five: five o'clock • **were to:** had the intention of + -ing
cross: traverse the Channel • **the Continent:** Europe
entered: no *in* after the verb • **sitting-room:** salon, antichamber
close behind: immediately after • **couple:** two or three • **papers:** newspapers, not magazines • **threw down:** put negligently
brought in: came in carrying • **luggage:** baggage • **withdrew:** retired • **from the window:** to face Vincent • **where ... looking out:** after contemplating the view • **another:** a • **in each other's arms:** embracing
drew apart: separated

damn it all: expression of irritation • **it doesn't seem ... going to be:** apparently will never be • **alone:** without company
look like it: give that impression • **softly:** gently

proved to be: revealed that it was • **waiter:** servant • **bearing:** bringing • **drawing the latter:** moving the table • **up to:** near
cast a ... round: had a brief circular look at the room • **there were anything further:** they wanted something else

for tea: let's have tea • **cheerily:** with animation, good humour
anything wrong?: is there a problem?
bolt upright: rigid • **staring:** looking fixedly; stare *at* sb
dazed: stupefied • **deathly white:** mortally pale

took a quick step towards her: approached her rapidly
sweetheart: darling

For answer she held out the paper to him, her finger pointing to the headline.

Vincent took the paper from her. 'FAILURE OF HOBSON, JEKYLL AND LUCAS,' he read. The name of the big city firm conveyed nothing to him at the moment, though he had an irritating conviction in the back of his mind that it ought to do so. He looked inquiringly at Theo.

'Richard is Hobson, Jekyll and Lucas,' she explained.

'Your husband?'

'Yes.'

Vincent returned to the paper and read the bald information it conveyed carefully. Phrases such as 'sudden crash', 'serious revelations to follow', 'other houses affected' struck him disagreeably.

Roused by a movement, he looked up. Theo was adjusting her little black hat in front of the mirror. She turned at the movement he made. Her eyes looked steadily into his.

'Vincent – I must go to Richard.'

He sprang up.

'Theo – don't be absurd.'

She repeated mechanically:

'I must go to Richard.'

'But, my dear –'

She made a gesture towards the paper on the floor.

'That means ruin – bankruptcy. I can't choose this day of all others to leave him.'

'You had left him before you heard of this. Be reasonable!'

She shook her head mournfully.

'You don't understand. I must go to Richard.'

And from that he could not move her. Strange that a creature so soft, so pliant, could be so unyielding. After the first, she did not argue. She let him say what he had to say unhindered. He held her in his arms, seeking to break her will by enslaving her senses, but though her soft mouth returned his kisses, he felt in her something aloof and invincible that withstood all his pleadings.

He let her go at last, sick and weary of the vain endeavour. From pleading he had turned to bitterness,

for: in place of an • **held out:** showed him
pointing to: indicating • **headline:** title in big letters
failure: crash
City: City of London, centre of financial and commercial business
conveyed: evoked • **though:** in spite of the fact that
in the back of his mind: somewhere in his memory
inquiringly: as if asking a question
is: is the proprietor, the owner

returned to the paper: took the paper again • **bald:** simple
conveyed: contained • **carefully:** attentively • **phrases:** expressions • **to follow:** imminent • **houses:** firms • **struck:** impressed
roused: alerted • **looked up:** lifted his eyes • **adjusting:** arranging
in front of: facing
steadily: without hesitation, firmly fixed • **his:** his eyes
go: return
sprang up: stood up precipitously
absurd: stupid, ridiculous
mechanically: without emotion, as if her decision was inevitable
must: it is my duty, that is all

towards: in the direction of
means: signifies, has the consequence • **this day ... others:** this particular day • **leave:** abandon
heard of: were informed about
mournfully: miserably
must: note the repetitive *must* as an obsession
from that: from that decision • **move her:** change her mind
pliant: easy to be influenced • **unyielding:** resolute • **after the first:** first argument, discussion • **argue:** discuss
unhindered: without interrupting him • **seeking:** trying
enslaving: captivating
felt: perceived by intuition • **aloof:** inaccessible
withstood: resisted • **pleadings:** supplications
sick and weary: disgusted • **endeavour:** attempt, effort
turned to: adopted • **bitterness:** acrimony

reproaching her with never having loved him. That, too, she took in silence, without protest, her face, dumb and pitiful, giving the lie to his words. Rage mastered him in the end; he hurled at her every cruel word he could think of, seeking only to bruise and batter her to her knees.

At last the words gave out; there was nothing more to say. He sat, his head in his hands, staring down at the red pile carpet. By the door, Theodora stood, a black shadow with a white face.

It was all over.

She said quietly: 'Goodbye, Vincent.'

He did not answer.

The door opened – and shut again.

III

The Darrells lived in a house in Chelsea – an intriguing, old-world house, standing in a little garden of its own. Up the front of the house grew a magnolia tree, smutty, dirty, begrimed, but still a magnolia.

Theo looked up at it, as she stood on the doorstep some three hours later. A sudden smile twisted her mouth in pain.

She went straight to the study at the back of the house. A man was pacing up and down in the room – a young man, with a handsome face and a haggard expression.

He gave an ejaculation of relief as she came in.

'Thank God you've turned up, Theo. They said you'd taken your luggage with you and gone off out of town somewhere.'

'I heard the news and came back.'

Richard Darrell put an arm about her and drew her to the couch. They sat down upon it side by side. Theo drew herself free of the encircling arm in what seemed a perfectly natural manner.

'How bad is it, Richard?' she asked quietly.

'Just as bad as it can be – and that's saying a lot.'

reproaching: note reproach *with* • **that:** that reproach
took in: accepted • **dumb:** inexpressive
giving the lie to: in contradiction with • **mastered:** dominated
hurled at her: insulted her with
seeking: attempting • **to bruise and batter:** to make her suffer cruelly
to her knees: to obtain complete submission • **at last:** in the end
gave out: ceased • **staring:** looking fixedly • **pile:** soft, woollen
by: at • **shadow:** vague form
all over: completely finished
quietly: note the repetitive *quiet* about Theodora, always self-controlled and unyielding

Chelsea: fashionable district in the West of London • **old-world:** not modern • **standing:** situated • **of its own:** private • **front:** façade
grew: stood • **smutty, dirty, begrimed:** neglected and miserable
still: all the same
on the doorstep: at the entrance • **some:** about, approximately
later: after • **twisted:** distorted • **in pain:** showing distress

straight: directly • **study:** room used for reading, writing, etc.
pacing up and down: walking from one side to the other

ejaculation: exclamation • **relief:** deliverance
turned up: arrived • **they said:** I was told
gone off out of: quit • **town:** London
somewhere: to some other place
heard: heard of, knew about
about: around • **drew:** attracted
couch: sofa • **drew herself free of:** disengaged herself from
in what ... manner: in a gesture which seemed perfectly natural

how bad is it?: is the situation very serious, grave? • **as bad ... be:** as bad as possible; note comparative • **saying a lot:** means extremely serious

'Tell me!'

He began to walk up and down again as he talked. Theo sat and watched him. He was not to know that every now and then the room went dim, and his voice faded from her hearing, while another room in a hotel at Dover came clearly before her eyes.

Nevertheless she managed to listen intelligently enough. He came back and sat down on the couch by her.

'Fortunately,' he ended, 'they can't touch your marriage settlement. The house is yours also.'

Theo nodded thoughtfully.

'We shall have that at any rate,' she said. 'Then things will not be too bad? It means a fresh start, that is all.'

'Oh! Quite so. Yes.'

But his voice did not ring true, and Theo thought suddenly: 'There's something else. He hasn't told me everything.'

'There's nothing more, Richard?' she said gently. 'Nothing worse?'

He hesitated for just half a second, then: 'Worse? What should there be?'

'I don't know,' said Theo.

'It'll be all right,' said Richard, speaking more as though to reassure himself than Theo. 'Of course, it'll be all right.'

He flung an arm about her suddenly.

'I'm glad you're here,' he said. 'It'll be all right now that you're here. Whatever else happens, I've got you, haven't I?'

She said gently: 'Yes, you've got me.' And this time she left his arm round her.

He kissed her and held her close to him, as though in some strange way he derived comfort from her nearness.

'I've got you, Theo,' he said again presently, and she answered as before: 'Yes, Richard.'

He slipped from the couch to the floor at her feet.

'I'm tired out,' he said fretfully. 'My God, it's been a day. Awful! I don't know what I should do if you weren't here. After all, one's wife is one's wife, isn't she?'

She did not speak, only bowed her head in assent.

tell me: let me know
as: during the time that
watched: observed • **he was not to:** it was impossible for him to
went dim: became indistinct • **his voice ... hearing:** the sound of his voice diminished • **while:** at the same time that • **came ... her eyes:** appeared clearly
nevertheless: in spite of that • **managed ... enough:** successfully tried to give intelligent attention to his speech
fortunately: providentially
settlement: contract • **yours also:** equally your property
nodded: approved with her head • **thoughtfully:** pensively
at any rate: in any case • **things:** the situation
a fresh start: the beginning of a new life
quite so: exactly
ring true: sound authentic
something else: another thing, another problem

worse: more unpleasant; note *worse*: bad to a greater degree
for: during • **half a second:** a little moment • **what should there be?:** why do you suppose there is more unpleasantness to come?

all right: satisfactory, ok • **as though to:** as if he wanted to

flung ... about her: embraced her
glad: pleased, happy
whatever else happens: in spite of possible new episodes

you've got me: you can count on me, rely on me
round: encircling
close to: in contact with, against
way: sort • **derived:** obtained, found • **nearness:** intimacy
presently: after a moment

slipped: moved quickly • **floor:** parquet
tired out: extremely fatigued • **fretfully:** nervously • **a day:** a long day • **awful:** horrible • **should:** conditional
one's wife: a man's wife, a married woman for better or worse
bowed her head: nodded • **assent:** approbation

He laid his head on her lap. The sigh he gave was like that of a tired child.

Theo thought again: 'There's something he hasn't told me. What is it?'

Mechanically her hand dropped to his smooth, dark head, and she stroked it gently, as a mother might comfort a child.

Richard murmured vaguely:

'It'll be all right now you're here. You won't let me down.'

His breathing grew slow and even. He slept. Her hand still smoothed his head.

But her eyes looked steadily into the darkness in front of her, seeing nothing.

'Don't you think, Richard,' said Theodora, 'that you'd better tell me everything?'

It was three days later. They were in the drawing room before dinner.

Richard started, and flushed.

'I don't know what you mean,' he parried.

'Don't you?'

He shot a quick glance at her.

'Of course there are – well – details.'

'I ought to know everything, don't you think, if I am to help?'

He looked at her strangely.

'What makes you think I want you to help?'

She was a little astonished.

'My dear Richard, I'm your wife.'

He smiled suddenly, the old, attractive, carefree smile.

'So you are, Theo. And a very good-looking wife, too. I never could stand ugly women.'

He began walking up and down the room, as was his custom when something was worrying him.

'I won't deny you're right in a way,' he said presently. 'There is something.'

He broke off.

laid: placed • **lap:** knees • **sigh:** exhalation • **gave:** emitted • **like that:** similar to the sigh

dropped: went down and touched • **smooth:** soft, delicate
stroked: caressed • **gently:** tenderly • **comfort:** console

won't let me down: will not abandon me

breathing: respiration • **grew:** became • **slow:** calm • **even:** regular • **smoothed:** caressed, stroked
steadily: fixedly • **darkness:** obscurity
seeing nothing: completely absent, in the void

you'd better: it would be reasonable to, it would be better for you to

later: after • **drawing room:** living room, salon

started: made a sudden movement of alarm • **flushed:** became red in the face • **mean:** insinuate • **parried:** answered evasively
don't you?: really?
shot a quick glance at her: gave her a brief look
well: expression of hesitation
I ought to: it would be preferable for me to • **I am to:** I must
help: aid

want you to: desire your help
astonished: surprised

old: familiar • **attractive:** charming • **carefree:** jovial, cheerful
so you are: yes, you are my wife • **good-looking:** beautiful
stand: tolerate • **ugly:** unattractive
walking up and down: (cf p. 84) expressing his anxiety
custom: habitual practice • **worrying him:** causing him anxiety
won't deny: must admit • **you're right:** it is the case • **in a way:** in a certain manner
broke off: stopped suddenly

'Yes?'

'It's so damned hard to explain things of this kind to women. They get hold of the wrong end of the stick – fancy a thing is – well, what it isn't.'

Theo said nothing.

'You see,' went on Richard, 'the law's one thing, and right and wrong are quite another. I may do a thing that's perfectly right and honest, but the law wouldn't take the same view of it. Nine times out of ten, everything pans out all right, and the tenth time you – well, hit a snag.'

Theo began to understand. She thought to herself: 'Why am I not surprised? Did I always know, deep down, that he wasn't straight?'

Richard went on talking. He explained himself at unnecessary lengths. Theo was content for him to cloak the actual details of the affair in this mantle of verbosity. The matter concerned a large tract of South African property. Exactly what Richard had done, she was not concerned to know. Morally, he assured her, everything was fair and above board; legally – well, there it was; no getting away from the fact, he had rendered himself liable to criminal prosecution.

He kept shooting quick glances at his wife as he talked. He was nervous and uncomfortable. And still he excused himself and tried to explain away that which a child might have seen in its naked truth. Then finally in a burst of justification, he broke down. Perhaps Theo's eyes, momentarily scornful, had something to do with it. He sank down in a chair by the fireplace, his head in his hands.

'There it is, Theo,' he said brokenly. 'What are you going to do about it?'

She came over to him with scarcely a moment's pause and, kneeling down by the chair, put her face against his.

'What can be done, Richard? What can we do?'

He caught her to him.

'You mean it? You'll stick to me?'

'Of course. My dear, of course.'

He said, moved to sincerity in spite of himself: 'I'm a

damned hard: terribly difficult • **kind:** sort
get ... stick: have a distorted perception of a problem • **fancy:** imagine • **a thing:** that a fact • **what it isn't:** what it is not in reality

law: justice • **right and wrong:** moral dignity or indignity
quite another: completely different • **may:** indicates possibility
right: regular • **take the same view:** have the same apprehension
pans out all right: reaches a satisfactory conclusion
hit a snag: meet an obstacle
thought to herself: reflected silently
deep down: in my profound consciousness
straight: honest

went on talking: continued to talk • **at unnecessary lengths:** interminably • **cloak:** cover • **actual:** real
mantle of verbosity: torrent of words • **matter:** affair
concerned: was about • **tract:** surface, part
concerned: interested
fair: correct • **above board:** absolutely regular
there it was: this was the situation • **no getting away:** impossible to escape • **liable:** subject by law • **criminal prosecution:** judgement for illegal act • **kept:** continued
uncomfortable: embarrassed • **still:** all the same
explain away: justify • **that which:** something that
in its naked truth: as evident • **burst:** explosion
broke down: lost control of himself, cracked up • **scornful:** showing disdain • **sank down:** let himself fall

there it is: that is all • **brokenly:** speaking with difficulty

scarcely: only just, barely • **pause:** hesitation
kneeling down: going on her knees • **put her face against his:** was face to face with him

caught: with his hand, forced her to approach
you mean it: are you serious

moved to sincerity: rendered sincere

thief, Theo. That's what it means, shorn of fine language – just a thief.'

'Then I'm a thief's wife, Richard. We'll sink or swim together.'

They were silent for a little while. Presently Richard recovered something of his jaunty manner.

'You know, Theo, I've got a plan, but we'll talk of that later. It's just on dinner-time. We must go and change. Put on that creamy thingummybob of yours, you know – the Caillot model.'

Theo raised her eyebrows quizzically.

'For an evening at home?'

'Yes, yes, I know. But I like it. Put it on, there's a good girl. It cheers me up to see you looking your best.'

Theo came down to dinner in the Caillot. It was a creation in creamy brocade, with a faint pattern of gold running through it and an undernote of pale pink to give warmth to the cream. It was cut daringly low in the back, and nothing could have been better designed to show off the dazzling whiteness of Theo's neck and shoulders. She was truly now a magnolia flower.

Richard's eye rested upon her in warm approval. 'Good girl. You know, you look simply stunning in that dress.'

They went in to dinner. Throughout the evening Richard was nervous and unlike himself, joking and laughing about nothing at all, as if in a vain attempt to shake off his cares. Several times Theo tried to lead him back to the subject they had been discussing before, but he edged away from it.

Then suddenly, as she rose to go to bed, he came to the point.

'No, don't go yet. I've got something to say. You know, about this miserable business.'

She sat down again.

He began talking rapidly. With a bit of luck, the whole thing could be hushed up. He had covered his tracks fairly well. So long as certain papers didn't get into the receiver's hands –

He stopped significantly.

thief: criminal • **means:** expresses • **shorn:** denuded • **fine:** refined
sink or swim: fail or succeed

while: moment • **presently:** after a pause
recovered: regained • **something:** a little • **jaunty:** carefree, relaxed
talk of: discuss
on dinner-time: time for dinner • **put on:** have on you
thingummybob of yours: your "thing" • **Caillot model:** dress made by the couturier Caillot
raised ... quizzically: had an expression of surprise on her face
evening at home: a simple soirée just you and me
there's a good girl: be a nice girl
cheers me up: consoles me • **your best:** at your advantage
in the Caillot: with the Caillot model on her
with a faint ... through it: decorated with a fluid motif of gold
undernote: imperceptible touch • **warmth:** vivacity
cut: open • **daringly:** audaciously
designed: conceived • **show off:** accentuate • **dazzling:** superb
neck and shoulders: *décolleté*

warm approval: enthusiastic approbation
stunning: fantastic • **dress:** *robe*
in: in the dining-room • **throughout:** during all
unlike: different from • **joking and laughing:** full of gaiety
attempt: effort • **shake off:** escape from
lead him back: make him come back
edged away from it: avoided it adroitly
rose: stood up • **bed:** her bedroom for the night
point: subject of conversation
don't go yet: stay one minute
miserable business: lamentable affair

bit of luck: minimum of good fortune • **hushed up:** dissimulated
covered ... well: made his traces indetectable • **so long as:** on condition that • **receiver:** administrator of fraudulent bankrupts

significantly: in order to attract attention to his insinuations

'Papers?' asked Theo perplexedly. 'You mean you will destroy them?'

Richard made a grimace.

'I'd destroy them fast enough if I could get hold of them. That's the devil of it all!'

'Who has them, then?'

'A man we both know – Vincent Easton.'

A very faint exclamation escaped Theo. She forced it back, but Richard had noticed it.

'I've suspected he knew something of the business all along. That's why I've asked him here a good bit. You may remember that I asked you to be nice to him?'

'I remember,' said Theo.

'Somehow I never seem to have got on really friendly terms with him. Don't know why. But he likes you. I should say he likes you a good deal.'

Theo said in a very clear voice: 'He does.'

'Ah!' said Richard appreciatively. 'That's good. Now you see what I'm driving at. I'm convinced that if you went to Vincent Easton and asked him to give you those papers, he wouldn't refuse. Pretty woman, you know – all that sort of thing.'

'I can't do that,' said Theo quickly.

'Nonsense.'

'It's out of the question.'

The red came slowly out in blotches on Richard's face. She saw that he was angry.

'My dear girl, I don't think you quite realize the position. If this comes out, I'm liable to go to prison. It's ruin – disgrace.'

'Vincent Easton will not use those papers against you. I am sure of that.'

'That's not quite the point. He mayn't realize that they incriminate me. It's only taken in conjunction with – with my affairs – with the figures they're bound to find. Oh! I can't go into details. He'll ruin me without knowing what he's doing unless somebody puts the position before him.'

'You can do that yourself, surely. Write to him.'

mean: want to say
destroy: eliminate

I'd: I would • **fast enough:** very rapidly • **get hold of:** take possession of • **devil:** the enormous difficulty
then: in that case
both: you and I
faint: ≠ loud • **escaped:** was emitted involuntarily
back (forced it): repressed it • **noticed:** observed
all along: since the origin, from the beginning
asked: invited • **a good bit:** frequently
remember: have in memory • **nice:** agreeable

somehow: for a reason or another • **got:** been • **on friendly terms:** in amicable relations • **likes:** appreciates
a good deal: enormously
he does: yes, I know that
appreciatively: with approbation, gratitude
I'm driving at: my intention is • **to:** to see

pretty: attractive, charming • **all that sort of thing:** many other things of the same sort, et cetera (not insisting on the details)
quickly: instantly
nonsense: this is ridiculous

the red ... blotches: red marks appeared little by little
angry: furious
quite: completely • **realize:** are conscious of • **the position:** my situation • **comes out:** is revealed
disgrace: dishonour
use: take advantage of • **against:** to attack

quite: exactly • **point:** problem
taken: considered • **conjunction:** connection
figures: traces of money • **are bound to find:** will discover inevitably • **without** + -ing
unless: except if • **puts ... him:** explains the situation to him

'A fat lot of good that would be! No, Theo, we've only got one hope. You're the trump card. You're my wife. You must help me. Go to Easton tonight –'

A cry broke from Theo.

'Not tonight. Tomorrow perhaps.'

'My God, Theo, can't you realize things? Tomorrow may be too late. If you could go now – at once – to Easton's rooms.' He saw her flinch, and tried to reassure her. 'I know, my dear girl, I know. It's a beastly thing to do. But it's life or death. Theo, you won't fail me? You said you'd do anything to help me –'

Theo heard herself speaking in a hard, dry voice. 'Not this thing. There are reasons.'

'It's life or death, Theo. I mean it. See here.'

He snapped open a drawer of the desk and took out a revolver. If there was something theatrical about that action, it escaped her notice.

'It's that or shooting myself. I can't face the racket. If you won't do as I ask you, I'll be a dead man before morning. I swear to you solemnly that that's the truth.'

Theo gave a low cry. 'No, Richard, not that!'

'Then help me.'

He flung the revolver down on the table and knelt by her side. 'Theo my darling – if you love me – if you've ever loved me – do this for me. You're my wife, Theo, I've no one else to turn to.'

On and on his voice went, murmuring, pleading. And at last Theo heard her own voice saying: 'Very well – yes.'

Richard took her to the door and put her into a taxi.

a fat ... would be: an excellent result that would produce (= no result at all) • **trump card:** master card, best resource

a cry broke from Theo: Theo exclaimed with anguish
perhaps: possibly

late: tardy • **at once:** immediately
rooms: residence, flat • **flinch:** make a nervous movement of aversion • **beastly:** repugnant • **life or death:** vital
fail: abandon • **anything:** all that is possible to do

hard: abrupt • **dry:** without emotion • **this thing:** to go in person for the papers • **there are reasons:** I have my reasons

snapped open: opened brusquely • **desk:** *bureau* • **took out:** extracted • **theatrical:** melodramatic
it escaped her notice: it did not attract her attention
shooting myself: committing suicide • **face the racket:** be confronted with publicity, notoriety
swear ... solemnly: make the solemn promise • **truth:** exact reality
low: practically inaudible

flung ... down: let fall violently • **knelt:** on his knees as if he was praying • **ever:** at any time
no one else: not another person, nobody else
turn to: go to for help
on and on: continually • **his voice went:** he spoke • **at last:** in the end
took: accompanied

IV

'Theo!'

Vincent Easton sprang up in incredulous delight. She stood in the doorway. Her wrap of white ermine was hanging from her shoulders. Never, Easton thought, had she looked so beautiful.

'You've come after all.'

She put out a hand to stop him as he came towards her.

'No, Vincent, this isn't what you think.'

She spoke in a low, hurried voice.

'I'm here from my husband. He thinks there are some papers which may – do him harm. I have come to ask you to give them to me.'

Vincent stood very still, looking at her. Then he gave a short laugh.

'So that's it, is it? I thought Hobson, Jekyll and Lucas sounded familiar the other day, but I couldn't place them at the minute. Didn't know your husband was connected with the firm. Things have been going wrong there for some time. I was commissioned to look into the matter. I suspected some underling. Never thought of the man at the top.'

Theo said nothing. Vincent looked at her curiously.

'It makes no difference to you, this?' he asked. 'That – well, to put it plainly, that your husband's a swindler?'

She shook her head.

'It beats me,' said Vincent. Then he added quietly: 'Will you wait a minute or two? I will get the papers.'

Theo sat down in a chair. He went into the other room. Presently he returned and delivered a small package into her hand.

'Thank you,' said Theo. 'Have you a match?'

Taking the matchbox he proffered, she knelt down by the fireplace. When the papers were reduced to a pile of ashes, she stood up.

'Thank you,' she said again.

'Not at all,' he answered formally. 'Let me get you a taxi.'

sprang up: jumped to his feet • **delight:** joy
doorway: entrance • **wrap:** cape, stole • **hanging from:** draped on • **never ... looked:** she had never looked (emphasis placed on *never*); note the inversion: *had she*

put out: extended • **towards her:** to meet her

hurried: urgent
from: acting in place of • **some:** certain

very still: immobile like a statue, petrified
short laugh: a dry sound of derision
so: introducing a conclusion • **that's it:** it is that, in reality
sounded: seemed (when heard) • **place:** situate
the minute: that moment • **connected:** associated
going wrong: deteriorating • **for some:** since a certain
commissioned: designated • **look into:** make investigations about
underling: inferior employee • **at the top:** of the most important rank • **curiously:** with curiosity
makes no difference: does not change anything
well: marking hesitation • **plainly:** clearly • **a swindler:** a man who practises malversations • **shook her head:** moved her head in disapproval • **beats:** stupefies • **quietly:** ≠ nervously
wait: stay here

presently: after a short time • **delivered:** deposited

match: for lighting a fire
proffered: offered • **by:** in front of
ashes: powdery residue left after burning

not at all: it was a pleasure • **formally:** in a polite and distant manner • **let me:** used to make a polite offer of help

He put her into it, saw her drive away. A strange, formal little interview. After the first, they had not even dared look at each other. Well, that was that, the end. He would go away abroad, try and forget.

Theo leaned her head out of the window and spoke to the taxi driver. She could not go back at once to the house in Chelsea. She must have a breathing space. Seeing Vincent again had shaken her horribly. If only – if only. But she pulled herself up. Love for her husband she had none – but she owed him loyalty. He was down, she must stick by him. Whatever else he might have done, he loved her; his offence had been committed against society, not against her.

The taxi meandered on through the wide streets of Hampstead. They came out on the heath, and a breath of cool, invigorating air fanned Theo's cheeks. She had herself in hand again now. The taxi sped back towards Chelsea.

Richard came out to meet her in the hall.

'Well,' he demanded, 'you've been a long time.'

'Have I?'

'Yes – a very long time. Is it – all right?'

He followed her, a cunning look in his eyes. His hands were shaking.

'It's – it's all right, eh?' he said again.

'I burnt them myself.'

'Oh!'

She went on into the study, sinking into a big armchair. Her face was dead white and her whole body drooped with fatigue. She thought to herself: 'If only I could go to sleep now and never, never wake up again!'

Richard was watching her. His glance, shy, furtive, kept coming and going. She noticed nothing. She was beyond noticing.

'It went off quite all right, eh?'

'I've told you so.'

'You're sure they were the right papers? Did you look?'

'No.'

'But then –'

put her into: installed her • **drive away:** go away in the taxi
the first: initial exchange of looks • **dared:** had the courage to
that was that: it was finished • **go away abroad:** quit England, go to another country • **try and forget** (≠ remember) if possible
leaned: inclined • **window:** separating glass between her and the driver • **go back:** return
breathing space: a moment of respite • **seeing:** the fact of seeing
shaken: troubled • **pulled herself up:** interrupted her reverie
none: not at all • **owed him loyalty:** was obliged to be loyal to him
down: vulnerable, at a disadvantage • **whatever else:** in spite of other things • **offence:** transgression
against: in opposition to
meandered on: continued to navigate • **through:** along • **wide:** large • **came out:** emerged • **heath:** open space • **breath ... air:** fresh current of air • **fanned:** caressed • **in hand:** under control
sped back: returned rapidly
came out: went • **meet:** receive • **hall:** entrance
demanded: asked authoratively • **been:** taken
have I?: really?
all right: all arranged, settled
followed: went after • **cunning:** perfidious
shaking: trembling

burnt them: made ashes of them

went on into: continued (to walk) and entered • **sinking:** plunging
dead white: livid • **drooped:** wanted to fall
go to sleep: become inconscious
never wake up again: never regain consciousness, die
watching: examining • **glance:** look • **shy:** timid • **kept coming and going:** moved continually • **beyond noticing:** now incapable (fatigue, disgust) of attention
went off: functioned
so: exactly that
right: authentic • **look:** verify

then: in that case

'I'm sure, I tell you. Don't bother me, Richard. I can't bear any more tonight.'

Richard shifted nervously.

'No, no. I see.'

He fidgeted about the room. Presently he came over to her, laid a hand on her shoulder. She shook it off.

'Don't touch me.' She tried to laugh. 'I'm sorry, Richard. My nerves are on edge. I feel I can't bear to be touched.'

'I know. I understand.'

Again he wandered up and down.

'Theo,' he burst out suddenly. 'I'm damned sorry.'

'What?' She looked up, vaguely startled.

'I oughtn't to have let you go there at this time of night. I never dreamed that you'd be subjected to any – unpleasantness.'

'Unpleasantness?' She laughed. The word seemed to amuse her. 'You don't know! Oh, Richard, you don't know!'

'I don't know what?'

She said very gravely, looking straight in front of her: 'What this night has cost me.'

'My God! Theo! I never meant – You – you did that, for me? The swine! Theo – Theo – I couldn't have known. I couldn't have guessed. My God!'

He was kneeling by her now stammering, his arms round her, and she turned and looked at him with faint surprise, as though his words had at last really penetrated to her attention.

'I – I never meant –'

'You never meant what, Richard?'

Her voice startled him.

'Tell me. What was it that you never meant?'

'Theo, don't let us speak of it. I don't want to know. I want never to think of it.'

She was staring at him, wide awake now, with every faculty alert. Her words came clear and distinct:

'You never meant – What do you think happened?'

'It didn't happen, Theo. Let's say it didn't happen.'

And still she stared, till the truth began to come to her.

tell: assure • **bother:** torment
bear: endure • **any more:** more fatigue
shifted: moved here and there

fidgeted about: turned round and round impatiently • **came over to:** approached • **laid:** put • **shook it off:** disengaged it nervously • **I'm sorry:** excuse me
my nerves are on edge: I am very nervous and irritable • **bear:** tolerate
wandered: walked without objective
burst out: exclaimed • **damned:** extremely
looked up: "up" indicates she was sitting
I oughtn't to have: I should not have • **let you go:** send you
dreamed: imagined • **subjected:** submitted
unpleasantness: disagreeable experience

straight: right, exactly

my God: expresses surprise and anger • **meant:** intended
swine: disgusting man • **I couldn't have known:** it was not possible for me to know • **guessed:** imagined, supposed
stammering: speaking in a hesitant manner
faint: ≠ great
as though his words ... attention: as if she was beginning to realize the sense of the words he used
meant: had the intention (mean, meant, meant)

what was it: what situation was it • **meant:** planned
don't let us: negative imperative 1st person plural • **I don't want to know:** I do not oblige you to confess
wide awake: totally conscious • **every faculty:** all her mental faculties • **alert:** vigilant • **came:** were pronounced
what do you think happened: what event do you suspect
it: the thing I don't want to know
come to her: appear clearly to her

'You think that –'

'I don't want –'

She interrupted him: 'You think that Vincent Easton asked a price for those letters? You think that I – paid him?'

Richard said weakly and unconvincingly: 'I – I never dreamed he was that kind of man.'

V

'Didn't you?' She looked at him searchingly. His eyes fell before hers. 'Why did you ask me to put on this dress this evening? Why did you send me there alone at this time of night? You guessed he – cared for me. You wanted to save your skin – save it at any cost – even at the cost of my honour.' She got up.

'I see now. You meant that from the beginning – or at least you saw it as a possibility, and it didn't deter you.'

'Theo –'

'You can't deny it. Richard, I thought I knew all there was to know about you years ago. I've known almost from the first that you weren't straight as regards the world. But I thought you were straight with me.'

'Theo –'

'Can you deny what I've just been saying?'

He was silent, in spite of himself.

'Listen, Richard. There is something I must tell you. Three days ago when this blow fell on you, the servants told you I was away – gone to the country. That was only partly true. I had gone away with Vincent Easton –'

Richard made an inarticulate sound. She held out a hand to stop him.

'Wait. We were at Dover. I saw a paper – I realized what had happened. Then, as you know, I came back.'

She paused.

Richard caught her by the wrist. His eyes burnt into hers.

'You came back – in time.'

you think that: she forces him to reveal his suspicion
I don't want: he insists that she is not obliged to confess

price: compensation • **paid:** recompensed him
weakly and unconvincingly: without any conviction
kind: type

searchingly: with penetrating eyes • **his eyes ... hers:** he looked at her for one moment only • **dress:** the Caillot model
alone: without you • **time:** hour
cared: had affection
skin: life • **cost:** price

see: understand • **meant:** planned • **at least:** at the minimum
saw: considered • **deter:** dissuade

deny: refute • **all there was to know:** everything
years ago: since a very long time • **almost:** practically
straight: scrupulous • **as regards:** concerning • **the world:** society

just: exactly, at this moment
in spite of himself: although he wanted to justify himself

this blow fell on you: you received this shock
was away: absent • **country:** rural place • **partly:** not entirely
gone away with: abandoned you to live with
held out: extended
stop him: keep him silent
wait: let me finish • **paper:** like *The Times*, *The Daily Mail*, etc.
happened: taken place

caught: seized • **wrist:** *poignet* • **his eyes burnt into hers:** he fixed her with eyes inflamed with passion
in time: before "it", cf p. 103

Theo gave a short, bitter laugh.

'Yes, I came back, as you say, 'in time', Richard.'

Her husband relinquished his hold on her arm. He stood by the mantelpiece, his head thrown back. He looked handsome and rather noble.

'In that case,' he said, 'I can forgive.'

'I cannot.'

The two words came crisply. They had the semblance and the effect of a bomb in the quiet room. Richard started forward, staring, his jaw dropped with an almost ludicrous effect.

'You – er – what did you say, Theo?'

'I said I cannot forgive! In leaving you for another man, I sinned – not technically, perhaps, but in intention, which is the same thing. But if I sinned, I sinned through love. You, too, have not been faithful to me since our marriage. Oh, yes, I know. That I forgave, because I really believed in your love for me. But the thing you have done tonight is different. It is an ugly thing, Richard – a thing no woman should forgive. You sold me, your own wife, to purchase safety!'

She picked up her wrap and turned towards the door.

'Theo,' he stammered out, 'where are you going?'

She looked back over her shoulder at him.

'We all have to pay in this life, Richard. For my sin I must pay in loneliness. For yours – well, you gambled with the thing you love, and you have lost it!'

'You are going?'

She drew a long breath.

'To freedom. There is nothing to bind me here.'

He heard the door shut. Ages passed, or was it a few minutes? Something fluttered down outside the window – the last of the magnolia petals, soft, fragrant.

short laugh: cf p. 99 • **bitter:** caustic

relinquished his hold on: disengaged
by the mantelpiece: near the fireplace • **thrown back:** in a rigid position, like a statue (throw, threw, thrown)
rather: restrictive; a little noble • **forgive:** *pardonner*

crisply: abruptly • **semblance:** resemblance
quiet: silent • **started forward:** had a sudden movement towards her
his jaw dropped: his mouth opened with incredulity • **ludicrous:** ridiculous

leaving: abandoning
sinned: committed a sin, an immoral action
through: caused by, for, due to
faithful: constant, loyal
forgave: pt of forgive • **really believed ... for me:** was really persuaded that you loved me
ugly: hideous, odious • **should:** moral obligation
sold: offered as merchandise • **to purchase safety:** in exchange for your impunity • **picked up:** seized • **wrap:** cf p. 99
stammered: pronounced with a stammer
looked back ... at him: turned her head to look at him
this life: our terrestrial existence
loneliness: solitude • **yours:** your sin • **gambled:** speculated
lost: ceased to possess

drew a long breath: respired profoundly
freedom: liberty • **bind:** attach
heard ... shut: perceived the sound of the door click • **ages:** a very long time • **a few:** a small number of • **fluttered:** floated • **the last:** the ultimate • **soft, fragrant:** cf p. 73

VOCABULARY

A

abject servile
about autour de, sur, au sujet de
above au-dessus
abroad (à) l'étranger
abrupt bourru
absurd ridicule, stupide
account for justifier de
across à travers, en travers de, de l'autre côté
actual réel, véritable
actually en réalité, vraiment
adjust se mettre
advertising publicitaire ; publicité
affair (love) liaison
afraid (be) craindre
after all après tout
again à nouveau
against contre
age vieillir
ages un siècle, une éternité
ahead of devant
air faire connaître
airman aviateur
alert vigilant
alight brillant
all agog (to see) curieux (de voir)
all along depuis le début
all right bien, sans problème, d'accord, OK
allude (to) faire allusion (à)
almost presque
alone seul
Alsatian berger allemand
although bien que
always toujours
amazed ébahi, stupéfait
amazement stupéfaction
amazing ahurissant
amidst parmi
amongst parmi
anger colère
angrily avec colère
angry en colère
annoying ennuyeux, irritant
answer for (have to) avoir des comptes à rendre
antique shop magasin d'antiquités
any ... more (not) ne ... plus
anything n'importe quoi
appeal to s'adresser à
appreciation satisfaction
appreciatively avec gratitude
approval approbation
argue discuter, argumenter
arm bras
armchair fauteuil
arouse soulever
arrow flèche (signalisation)
as au moment où, comme, pendant que
as far as aussi loin que
as though comme si
as yet jusqu'à maintenant
ash cendre
ask inviter
assent acquiescement, approbation
assurance conviction
astonished stupéfait
attempt essayer, tâter, tentative
attend to s'occuper de (un client), servir
attractive séduisant
averse to opposé à
avoid éviter
awake (wide) totalement réveillé
awake (awoke awoken) (s')éveiller
away loin de là
away parti, absent

awful terrible, épouvantable
awkward délicat

B

baby petit
back dos
back (at the) au fond de
bad mauvais
badly gravement, sérieusement
baffle déconcerter
baker boulanger
bald simple
bank rive
bantering badin
bare nu, sans ornement
barely à peine, tout juste
batter battre
battered décrépit
be after rechercher
be to aller (faire qch), devoir, falloir
be under one's thumb être sous la coupe de qq
beam rayonner (de joie)
bear (bore borne) (ap)porter
bear supporter
beast brute
beastliness cruauté, méchanceté
beastly abominable
beat battement
beat (beat beaten) battre, frapper
beats me (it) cela me dépasse
beautiful admirable
become (became become) devenir
bed lit
behave se conduire
behave (oneself) bien se conduire, être sage
behind derrière
belief conviction, foi
believe croire, penser
belong (to) appartenir (à)
bend (bent bent) se pencher
bend virage
beneath sous
bereaved endeuillé, affligé
beset (beset beset) assaillir
beside à côté de
best (for the) au mieux
best (look one's) être en beauté
best of le meilleur de
better mieux
better (had) ferait mieux de
between entre
bewildered perplexe
beyond au-delà, de l'autre côté
bind (bound bound) lier, attacher
bit morceau, passage
bit (a) un peu
bit (a good) fréquemment
bit (not a) pas du tout
bit of luck (a) une chance
bite (bit bitten) mordre
bitter acerbe, cinglant
bitterly amèrement
bitterness amertume
bleared voilés, troubles (yeux)
blink cligner (des yeux)
blood sang
bloom floraison
blooming éclatant (beauté), sacré, foutu
blotch tache
blow coup, choc
blush rougir
board (above) régulier, dans les règles
body corps, cadavre
bolt foncer, se précipiter
bolt upright droit comme un i
bone os
boracic acide borique
bore ennuyer
both à la fois, tous les deux
bother harceler, se faire du souci
bother (with) s'embarrasser (de qq)
bottom fond

bound sûr, certain
bow pencher, incliner
boyhood enfance
break (broke broken) (se) briser, casser
break (news) annoncer
break down s'effondrer
break into commencer
break off s'arrêter net, s'interrompre
breath souffle
breath (draw a long) respirer à fond
breathe respirer
breathing respiration, souffle
breathing space moment de répit
breathless hors d'haleine, essoufflé
breeding bonnes manières
bribery corruption
bride jeune mariée
bridge pont
bring (brought brought) apporter
bring back ramener
bring in apporter
bring up élever, éduquer, évoquer
broad large
broad-shouldered large d'épaules
brocade brocart
broken up brisé, déprimé
brokenly d'une voix entrecoupée
brood ruminer
brother frère
brow front
brows sourcils
bruise meurtrir
build (built built) construire
bulb bulbe (de plante)
bump cahoter
burn (burnt burnt) brûler, hâler
burst (burst burst) éclater, exploser
burst explosion
burst out s'exclamer, s'écrier
bush broussailles, taillis
business affaire, histoire
bust (to do a) faire la course
bustle remue-ménage
busy occupé
buy (bought bought) acheter
by devant, à côté de
by (oneself) seul

C

call visite
call appeler, rendre visite
call to s'adresser à
can (could) pouvoir
card-case paquet-cadeau
care about être attaché à
care aimer bien
care for prêter attention à
carefree insouciant
careful méticuleux, attentif
carefully soigneusement
caretaker gardien
carry (trans)porter
case coffret
case (in any) de toute façon
cast (cast cast) jeter
cast aside rejeter
cast down baisser
casually fortuitement, en passant
cat chameau, rosse (femme)
cat (old) vieille rosse
catch (caught caught) saisir, attraper, comprendre
catch sb's eyes attirer l'attention de qq
cave antre, repaire
challenge mettre au défi
chance hasard, occasion
change changement
chap type, homme
character personnage
charge (in) responsable
chase (hunting) chasse à courre
chasten calmer, assagir

cheap bon marché, sans valeur
check oneself se retenir
cheek joue
cheer up prendre courage, remonter le moral
cheerful joyeux
cheerily gaiement, avec entrain
cheering encourageant
chemist pharmacien
chemist's shop pharmacie
cherry cerise
childhood enfance
choose (chose chosen) choisir
circle tourner
civil-spoken courtois (langage)
clad vêtu
claim revendiquer
clasp agrafer, attacher
clever habile, intelligent
cleverness habileté
cling (clung clung) coller, adhérer
cling (on sb) dépendre de
clinging enlacement
cloak masquer, déguiser
close enclos, renfermé (air)
close (up) (tout) près
closely fermement
clothes vêtements
clouded nuageux
clue indice
clutch (s')agripper
coarsen durcir
cold shiver sueur froide
coloured de couleur, noir
come (came come) venir, arriver
come along venir
come and go aller et venir
come back revenir
come by obtenir, se procurer
come out aboutir à, atteindre, apparaître, se révéler
come round visiter
come to reprendre conscience
comfort consoler
commissioned (be) être chargé d'enquêter
complacency complaisance
complain se plaindre
concerned soucieux
conduct conduite
confront faire face
congratulate féliciter
conjunction with (in) conjointement à
connect rattacher, associer
consider réfléchir à
content(ed) satisfait
contractor entrepreneur
convenient commode, opportun
convey communiquer, transmettre, dire, évoquer
cool frais
corner coin, endroit
cost prix, frais, dépense
costly coûteux, cher
couch canapé, divan
counter riposter
country campagne
county comté
couple deux ou trois
court cour
cover one's tracks brouiller les pistes
cracked fou, dérangé
crash fracasser
craziness folie
crazy fou, détraqué
creamy crémeux
credit mérite
criminal relatif à un acte illégal
crisis moment critique
crisply tranchant, cassant
crook escroc
cross traverser
crossroads carrefour
crouch (down) ratatiner, recroqueviller
crumble s'écrouler
crutch béquille
cry out s'exclamer, crier
cunning rusé
curiously avec curiosité
curl boucle

curse malédiction, maudire
custom habitude
cut (cut cut) couper, tailler
cutting découpage (cinéma)

D

damn it all! bon sang !, nom de nom !
damned + adj très, terriblement
dare oser
dare say supposer
daringly audacieusement
dark brun (cheveux), sombre
darkness obscurité, ténèbres
darling chouchou, enfant chéri
dash mouvement brusque, élan
daughter-in-law bru, belle-fille
days (it's early) c'est le début
dazed hébété
dazzling éblouissant
dead mort
dead white pâle comme la mort, blafard
deal (dealt dealt) s'approvisionner
deal (a good) beaucoup, énormément
dear (a) un amour
death mort
deathly cadavérique
decay délabrement
deceiver menteur, trompeur
decidedly sans aucun doute
declare annoncer
deduce conclure
deed action
deep (colour) foncé
deep down au fin fond
defining définition
definitely certainement
deft habile, vif
deliberate réfléchir
delight grand plaisir, joie
delightful délicieux, charmant
deliver remettre
demand exiger, réclamer
deny nier, refuser d'admettre
depart partir
depth (be out of one's) se sentir dépassé
derelict en ruines
derive from puiser dans
deserted vide, désert
deserve mériter
design concevoir, créer
desk bureau, secrétaire
despise mépriser
destroy détruire
deter empêcher, dissuader
development rebondissement
devil diable
devoted attentionné
diamond diamant
die mourir
dim vague, incertain
dirt-cheap pour rien, donné
dirty sale, crasseux
disappoint décevoir
discouragingly d'un ton décourageant
disgrace honte, déshonneur
display afficher
distastefully avec dégoût
disturb déranger
divide up partager
dizziness vertige
do (did done) faire
do a bunk prendre la poudre d'escampette
dodge tour, truc
done up exténué
doorstep seuil (de porte)
doorway embrasure de porte
doubtfully avec doute, d'un air dubitatif
dower house maison familiale
down à terre
down here par ici
drab morne
draw (drew drawn) (at)tirer
draw (apart) se séparer
draw free se dégager
drawing-room salon
dread (dread dread) craindre

dream (dreamt dreamt) rêver, songer
dreamy songeur, rêveur
dress robe
drift s'écouler, passer lentement
drink (drank drunk) boire
drive (drove driven) conduire
drive trajet (en voiture)
drive at en venir à, vouloir dire
drive back retourner en voiture
drive to attirer, pousser vers
driver conducteur
driving conduite (auto)
drone ronronner (voix)
droop (s'a)baisser, (s')affaisser, courber
drop (laisser) tomber
drown noyer
dry sec, sécher
dull mat, terne, monotone
dumb muet
dumbly sans voix
dwell (dwelt dwelt) habiter, résider
dwell upon s'étendre, s'appesantir sur

E

each other l'un l'autre
eager ardent, enthousiaste
eagerly ardemment
early tôt
earn gagner (de l'argent)
ease facilité, aise
easily facilement
easy facile
eat (ate eaten) manger
ecstatically avec ravissement
edge (my nerves are on) j'ai les nerfs à vif
edge (teeth on) nerfs à vif
edge away s'éloigner furtivement
either chacun, chaque
ejaculation exclamation
elderly âgé
else (d')autre
else (sth) autre chose
elusive élusif, vague
embolden enhardir
emergency cas urgent, imprévu
empty vide, désert
end but, fin
end (at a loose) sans trop savoir quoi faire
endeavour effort
engage fiancer
engaging attirant, attachant
enjoy aimer, prendre plaisir à
enough assez
ensconced bien à l'abri
enslave asservir
entangle empêtrer
erstwhile d'autrefois, précédent
escape sb échapper à qq, n'être pas remarqué par qq
escape from échapper à
estate domaine, propriété
even même, régulier
evening soirée
event événement
ever jamais, toujours
every chaque, tous
everywhere partout
excitement agitation
exercise pratiquer, utiliser
expect s'attendre à, supposer
explain away justifier
explaining explication
exquisite raffiné, exquis
extend offrir, présenter
exultantly avec jubilation
eye œil
eyebrow sourcil
eyelid paupière

F

face faire face
facetiously en plaisantant
factory usine, fabrique
fade diminuer, s'affaiblir
fail abandonner, faire défaut
failure faillite
faint faible, léger, imperceptible

fair joli, juste, équitable
fairly très, assez
fairness beauté ; honnêteté
fairy fée, magique
faithful fidèle
fall (fell fallen) tomber
fall to se changer en
famous réputé
fan éventer
fancy (s')imaginer, supposer, se figurer
far above très supérieur
far-off lointain
far-reaching d'importance considérable
fashion façon, manière
fashionable à la mode
fast rapidement
fastness abri, refuge
fat lot of good (a) c'est fou ce que...
fear frayeur
feast (on) se régaler (de)
feel (felt felt) (se) sentir
feel like ressembler
feeling sentiment
fellow type, homme
fence recéleur
few (a) quelques
figure chiffre, silhouette, corps
fill remplir
find (found found) trouver, découvrir
fine délicat, raffiné
finger doigt
fire feu
fireplace feu, âtre
first (pour) la première fois
first (the) le début
fishy louche
fist poing
fix arriver à un arrangement
flame (old) ancien amant
flash éclair, étinceler
flashpot endroit luxueux
flat à plat
flaxen blond
flicker battre des cils
flinch tressaillir
fling (flung flung) projeter, lancer
fling one's arm about sb se jeter au cou de qq
float down tomber doucement
floor plancher
flow (flew flown) (s'en)voler
flu grippe
flush rougir, teint rose
fluster agitation
flutter s'agiter, papillonner, voleter, voltiger
fly (flew flown) voler
fly (up) lancer en l'air
focus concentrer
fold pli
follow suivre
following suivant
fond of (be) avoir de l'affection pour, aimer
fool idiot
foot (pl. feet) pied
footbrake pédale de frein
for car, parce que
for pendant
force back réprimer
forever pour toujours
forget (forgot forgotten) oublier
forgive (forgave forgiven) pardonner
formally cérémonieusement
fortitude force d'âme
fortnight quinzaine, deux semaines
fortunately heureusement
forward en avant
fourth quatrième
fragrance senteur
fragrant odorant
frame encadrer
freedom liberté
frenzied frénétique
fresh nouveau
fret se tourmenter
fretfully avec énervement

friendly amical
friendship amitié
frighten effrayer, faire peur
frightful effrayant
frock robe
from then on à partir de maintenant
front (in) devant
front façade
front door entrée (porte d')
frown froncer les sourcils
fruit fruits
frying pan poêle à frire
fulfil accomplir, réaliser
fundamentals principes essentiels
funk éviter
funny étrange, drôle
furniture meubles
furniture van camion de déménagement
further davantage, supplémentaire

G

gain atteindre, gagner, conquérir
gallantly courageusement
gamble miser, spéculer
gates portail
gaudily de façon clinquante
gaze regarder avec intensité
gear (in) en prise
genially aimablement
gently doucement
genuine authentique
get (got got) avoir, devenir
get away s'en aller
get back retourner, revenir, obtenir
get down déprimer
get hold of se procurer
get on réussir
get over surmonter
get through traverser
get to arriver à, en venir à
get up se lever
ghastly livide
ghoul goule, vampire
gift cadeau
girl (jeune) fille
give (gave given) donner
give out s'épuiser
give up abandonner
glad content, heureux
glance jeter un coup d'œil
glance up lever les yeux
glass verre
gleaming rutilant
glimpse coup d'œil
gloomy sinistre
glow lueur, rutiler, flamboyer
go (went gone) devenir, aller
go away s'en aller, partir
go back rentrer, retourner
go off réussir, fonctionner, partir
go on continuer
go out sortir, être invité
go through conclure
go wrong mal tourner
golden doré
good bien, bon
good-looking beau, belle
good looks beauté (visage)
good luck bonne chance
goods marchandise
gossip cancaner
grasp saisir
gratify satisfaire
greet saluer
grievance grief
grim menaçant
grin avoir un large sourire
grind (ground ground) grincer
ground floor rez-de-chaussée
grow (grew grown) grandir, (faire) pousser, devenir
grower producteur
grumble ronchonner
guess deviner

H

hack parcourir
had best (I) je ferais mieux de

hall vestibule, entrée
halt hésiter
hand occasion, « main »
handbrake frein à main
hand over passer, transmettre
handbag sac à main
handsome beau
handsomely généreusement
handy à portée de la main
hang (hung hung) (sus)pendre
hang together être cohérent, se tenir
hanker after aspirer à, rêver de
happen arriver, survenir
happiness bonheur
hard difficile, dur, difficilement
hardly à peine
harp rabâcher, répéter sans cesse
harshly avec brusquerie
hate haïr
have oneself in hand se contrôler
have to avoir à, devoir
headache mal de tête
headline manchette, gros titre
head-over-heels éperdument
headthing truc pour la tête
heap amas, pile
hear (heard heard) entendre
hear of entendre parler de, apprendre
hearing oreille, ouïe
heart cœur
heartily de bon cœur
hearty cordial
heat chaleur
heath lande
heavy lourd
help aider
help it (can I)? est-ce de ma faute?
hem border
highly hautement
highway route principale
hip hanche
hoarsely d'une voix rauque
hold (held held) tenir, serrer, (se) tenir, (se) cramponner
hold out (é)tendre, présenter
hold sb close serrer qq dans ses bras
hold with (not) ne pas être d'accord
honest(ly) honnêtement
hope espérer
house compagnie, maison de commerce
household equipment appareils ménagers
how comment
how goes it? comment cela va-t-il?
how many? combien?
huddled recroquevillé
huge énorme, gigantesque
hung (hang hang) (about) traîner, rôder
hurl jeter, lancer avec violence
hurried précipité, rapide
hurriedly en toute hâte
hurry se hâter
hurrying d'un pas pressé
hurt (hurt hurt) blesser
husband époux, mari
hush up étouffer, cacher

I

I can't help + ing je ne peux m'empêcher de
I do declare ça par exemple
illuminated coloré
ill-wish souhaiter du mal
imbue with imprégner de
impart communiquer
impudence insolence
impulse impulsion
inch (every) la moindre parcelle
incredulous incrédule
indeed en effet, réellement
indiscriminate sans discernement
injury blessure
inner intérieur

innuendo insinuation
inquiringly d'un air interrogateur
instead of au lieu de, à la place de
intent absorbé, attentif
interpolate interrompre
irresolutely avec hésitation

J

jaunty désinvolte
jaw mâchoire
jerk out éjecter brutalement
jest plaisanter
jewellery joaillerie
jewels bijoux
joke plaisanter
jolly drôlement, rudement
just now à l'instant, il y a un instant

K

keep (kept kept) garder
keep + -ing continuer à
kill tuer
kind espèce, sorte
kind(ly) gentil
kingdom royaume (de Dieu)
kiss baiser, effleurer
knee genou
kneel (knelt knelt) s'agenouiller
knock frapper
knowledge connaissance, savoir

L

labour main-d'œuvre
lack manque
land pays
lane chemin, sentier
lap genoux, giron
large grand
lash cil
last dernier, durer
last (at) enfin
lastly finalement
late tard
lately récemment
later plus tard
latest nouveau, dernier
latter dernier, deuxième
laugh (éclat de) rire
laughing riant, rieur
law loi, justice
lay (laid laid) poser, établir (un plan)
lead (led led) conduire, diriger
lead back ramener, revenir
leak fuir, prendre l'eau
lean mince, maigre
lean (leant leant) se pencher
lean back s'adosser
leap (sur)saut
leap (leapt leapt) bondir
least (at) au moins
least (nothing in the) rien du tout
leave (left left) laisser, quitter
leer regard mauvais
leisure loisir
leisureliness lenteur, pondération
leisurely calmement, lentement
length longueur
let (let let) louer
let sb down laisser tomber qq
liable to (be) risquer de, être passible de
lid couvercle
lie (lay lain) être étendu
lie mensonge
lie (to give the) démentir, contredire
lie back se renverser en arrière
life vie, existence
light allumer, léger
lightly avec légèreté, en plaisantant
like aimer bien, apprécier
like comme
likely probable
limp claudication

line (of least resistance) solution de facilité
linger s'attarder
link lier, unir
lip lèvre
listen to écouter
listless indolent
live vivre, habiter
loneliness solitude
lonely seul
long as (so) à condition que
look apparaître, sembler; expression
look after prendre soin de, suivre du regard
look into examiner
look like avoir l'air, ressembler
look out to donner, s'ouvrir sur
look up lever les yeux
Lord! Seigneur! Mon Dieu!
lose (lost lost) perdre
lot (a) beaucoup, très
lot (a lot of) un grand nombre de
lovely agréable, joli, excellent, succulent
lover amoureux
low bas
luck chance
ludicrous risible, ridicule
luggage bagages
luxuries objets de luxe

M

mad fou, dérangé
maid femme de chambre; **old ~** vieille fille
make (made made) faire
make good réussir
make out prétendre
make sense être logique, avoir un sens
malevolent maléfique
maliciously méchamment
manage réussir, parvenir
manner attitude, comportement
mansion demeure, petit manoir
mantelpiece cheminée
many (+ pl) beaucoup
many a plus d'un
marks (full) félicitations
master dominer
match allumette
matter affaire, matière, problème
matter (what does it)? qu'est-ce que cela fait?
may (might) pouvoir
mean (meant meant) signifier, vouloir dire
mean prévoir, représenter
meander serpenter
means of (by) au moyen de
mechanically machinalement
medicine médicament
meet (met met) rencontrer, accueillir
meet sb's eyes croiser le regard de qq
meeting-place lieu de rendez-vous
mention parler de
merriment hilarité
mid-speech au milieu d'une phrase
mind (make up one's) se décider
mind considérer, être contrarié, protester
mind esprit, pensée, intention, avis
mingle mêler
minute détaillé
miserable lamentable
mishap (without) sans encombre
miss manquer, rater
missing disparu
mistake (mistook mistaken) se tromper
misunderstand mal comprendre
moisten mouiller
money match mariage d'argent
mood disposition, humeur

mosquito netting moustiquaire
most très
mostly surtout
mothball boule de naphtaline
motoring en voiture
mournfully tristement
move bouger, faire bouger, pousser, inciter
move back retourner
move over se déplacer
much beaucoup
muck scandale, ordure
muffled étouffé (bruit, voix)
munch croquer, dévorer
murder assassiner
must devoir
mute silencieux
mutter marmonner

N

naked truth la vérité toute nue
nasty mauvais
nasty-looking l'air désagréable
near environ
nearly à peu près
nearness intimité
necklace collier
need avoir besoin de
needle aiguille
negotiate surmonter, franchir
neighbour voisin
neighbourhood quartier, voisinage
neither of them ni l'un ni l'autre
nerve courage
nervy énervé
never jamais
never mind ne t'en fais pas
nevertheless néanmoins, cependant
news nouvelle(s)
next ensuite, prochain, suivant
nice gentil, aimable
night nuit
nobody personne
nod hocher la tête
none aucun
nonsense absurdités, inepties
not ... any more ne ... plus
note remarquer
nothing rien
notice remarquer
notice (escape one's) ne pas s'apercevoir
now maintenant
now and then de temps en temps
now (up to) jusqu'à présent

O

obituary notice notice nécrologique
odd étrange, bizarre
offence délit, infraction
office bureau
old ancien, d'autrefois
old world désuet
on and on sans discontinuer
once autrefois, une fois
once (at) tout de suite, immédiatement
only seul, seulement
open ouvrir
opening gambit ruse, stratagème
opposite en face de
orchard verger
original initial
other autre
otherwise autrement
ought to devoir, falloir
ought to (I) je devrais, il faudrait que je
out dehors
out of (one ... fifty) un sur 50
output production
outraged furieux
outside au-dehors, de l'autre côté
over (adj) fini, là-bas, par-dessus, plus de
overgrown envahi
overpowering suffocant
owe devoir, être redevable

owing to grâce à, à cause de
owl hibou
own posséder
own (of its) particulier
owner propriétaire

P

pace up and down marcher de long en large
pain souffrance
pan out allright bien se passer, bien tourner
pang douleur
panic-stricken frappé de panique
paper journal
parlour-maid femme de chambre
parry éluder
part (on one's) de son côté
Parthian shot remarque acerbe, trait
partly en partie
pass passer devant
passage traversée
past devant
path chemin
pattern motif
pause arrêt, silence, s'interrompre, s'arrêter
pebble galet
peculiar rare, singulier
pension off renvoyer avec une pension
people gens
perhaps peut-être
peruse lire attentivement
phrase expression
pick choisir, cueillir
pick up ramasser, reprendre
pictures (the) le cinéma
pieces (all to) en miettes
pile carpet tapis de laine
pillow oreiller
pinch faucher, piquer, chiper ; arrêter, pincer
pinewood pinède
pink rose
pitch into tomber sur
pitiful pitoyable
place situer
plainly simplement, clairement
platform quai
plead prétexter
pleading prière, plaidoyer
plenty of beaucoup de
pliant docile
poach braconner
point question, essentiel
point out/to indiquer, montrer
poor pauvre
popular connu, aimé par beaucoup
porter porteur
position situation, position
posse troupe, armée
postpone ajourner
pour down se déverser, tomber
powder poudre
powerful puissant
presently bientôt
pretty délicat, joli
pretty + adj assez
prevent empêcher, éviter
proceed aller, circuler
proffer offrir, tendre
prominence importance
proper adéquat, approprié
prosecution poursuites judiciaires
proud fier
prove to be s'avérer
pry s'occuper de ce qui ne vous regarde pas
puff bouffée
pull tirer
pull down démolir
pull oneself together/up se ressaisir
purchase acheter
put (put put) poser, mettre
put an act jouer un rôle
put away ranger
put down attribuer

put on mettre (sur soi)
put on weight grossir
put out (one's hand) lever (la main)
puzzle embarrasser, rendre perplexe, énigme

Q

queer bizarre
quick rapide
quickly avec vivacité
quiet silencieux, tranquille
quietly discrètement
quite très, tout à fait
quite so tout à fait
quiver frémir
quizzically d'un air perplexe

R

rabbit lapin
racket grand bruit, vacarme
raise (é)lever
rank luxuriant
rapture extase
rapturous enchanté, délicieux
rate (at any) en tout cas
rather plutôt
rattle fracas, bruit de ferraille
reach arriver à, atteindre
reach up lever le bras pour atteindre
ready prêt
realize se rendre compte
really vraiment
reasonably assez
receiver administrateur judiciaire
recklessly avec témérité
record enregistrer
recover recouvrer, reprendre
reflection reflet, image
regal majestueux
regard considérer
regards (as) en ce qui concerne
regime situation
registered post recommandé
regular vrai, véritable
release (re)lâcher
relief soulagement
relinquish one's hold on sth (re)lâcher qch
remain rester
remember se souvenir de
remotest (the) le plus vague
remove enlever, ôter
reply répondre
repudiate rejeter, repousser
request demande
require nécessiter, demander
requisition réquisitionner (les services)
resent en vouloir à qq, ressentir de l'injustice
resource invention
response réponse, réaction
rest se reposer
retire prendre sa retraite
return remettre (à sa place) / refléter / rendre, restituer / revenir, retourner
reverently avec respect
rid (rid rid) (oneself) se débarrasser
rid of (be) être débarrassé de
ride (rode ridden) monter à cheval
right bien, exact
right (be) avoir raison
right up exactement
ring bague
ring (rang rung) sonner
ripe mûr
rise (rose risen) se lever, s'élever
rise to one's feet se mettre debout
roam (over) parcourir
rob voler, dérober
robbery vol
rolled into one tout à la fois
romance novel roman psychologique
roof toit
rooms appartement

rot (rot rotten) pourrir
rough violent
round autour, tout autour / de l'autre côté
roundly carrément
rouse alerter
run (ran run) courir
run (into debts) contracter (des dettes)
rush précipiter, hâter, se ruer
rush (with a) précipitamment
rut ornière

S

sable fur fourrure en martre, zibeline
sack (get the) être renvoyé
sadly tristement
safety sécurité
same même, pareil
same (all the) malgré tout
same (the) la même chose
same as (the) comme
save from éviter de
saying proverbe
scapegrace vaurien
scar cicatrice
scarcely à peine
scare effrayer, peur, frayeur
scathingly d'une manière cinglante, sarcastique
scene scène, querelle
scenery décor
scent parfum, odeur
scorching intense, extrême
scornful méprisant
scratch gratter
scream hurler
scrub broussailles
search chercher
searchingly de façon pénétrante
seat place, siège
see (saw seen) voir
seedling plante
seek (sought sought) chercher
seem avoir l'air
seldom rarement
self-reliant sûr de soi
sell (sold sold) vendre
semblance apparence
send (sent sent) envoyer
sense sens commun, bon sens
sensitive sensible
seraphic éthéré
set (set set) mettre ; sertir
set about se mettre à
set in survenir
settee canapé
settle calmer
settle régler, trancher
settle down se ranger, se calmer
settle in s'installer, emménager
settlement contrat
several plusieurs
shade ombre / teinte
shadow ombre
shady ombragé
shake (shook shaken) secouer ; hocher la tête (refus)
shake off repousser, se libérer de
shame honte
sharp aigu / insidieux / sévère, cinglant
sharply vivement
shed hangar
sheet feuille
shelter (s')abriter
shepherd guider, diriger
shield abriter, protéger
shift remuer, bouger
shine (shone shone) briller
shiver frisson / frissonner
shoot (shot shot) lancer
shoot (oneself) se tuer (d'une balle)
shoot through traverser brutalement
shorn off dépouillé de
short brusque, sec / court
shout crier, hurler
shove down appuyer en poussant

show (show, showed or shown) montrer
show off mettre en valeur
show up montrer du doigt
shrug (one's shoulders) hausser (les épaules)
shut (shut shut) se(re)fermer
shy faire un écart / timide
sick malade
side côté
side (by the side of) à côté de
sideways de côté
sigh soupir, soupirer
significantly de façon significative
silly stupide
silvery argenté
sin pécher, commettre un péché
since depuis
sink (sank sunk) sombrer, se laisser tomber
sink down s'affaisser
sink or swim s'en tirer, se débrouiller
sit (sat sat) être assis
sit up se redresser
sitting-room salon
size taille
skin peau
slam fermer bruyamment
sleep (go to) s'endormir
sleepwalker somnambule
slightly légèrement
slip (se) glisser
slip out s'éclipser
slip to tomber à, sur
slovenly bâclé, négligé
slow lent
slow down ralentir
slowly lentement
slumbering endormi, paisible
smell odeur
smile sourire
smooth lisse, doux / lisser
smoothness douceur, délicatesse
smutty noirci, taché
snag (hit a) tomber sur un os
snake serpent
snap open s'ouvrir bruyamment
snatch saisir brutalement, arracher
sniff renifler
snort hennir
so donc, tellement, si
soft souple
soften (se) radoucir
softly doucement
softness douceur
solicitous inquiet
solve résoudre
some environ, quelque, quelques
somehow d'une manière ou d'une autre, quelque peu
something quelque chose
something of quelque peu de
sometimes parfois
somewhat un peu, quelque peu
somewhere quelque part
soon bientôt
sorrow malheur, chagrin
sorry désolé
sort trier
sort of thing (all that) et tout ça
soul âme
sound bruit / sembler (à l'oreille)
southern du Sud
spare épargner
sparkle étinceler
speak (spoke spoken) dire, parler
speed (sped sped) aller à vive allure
spike sb's guns mettre des bâtons dans les roues de qq
spine colonne vertébrale
spinster vieille fille
spirit courage, caractère / énergie
spite of (in) malgré

spoil (spoilt spoilt) gâcher, gâter
spot endroit
spread (spread spread) (s')étaler, (s')étendre
spring (sprang sprung) jaillir
spring up se lever d'un bond
spunk courage, cran
squat être accroupi
squeeze (one's way) se frayer un chemin
stage (to go on the) faire du théâtre
stale renfermé, (air) vicié
stammer bégayer, balbutier
stamp duty droit de timbre
stand (stood stood) être debout / placer, situer / tolérer, supporter
stand over se tenir près de
stand up against combattre
stare regarder fixement
start commencer / départ, début / partir, s'en aller / tressaillir
start forward faire un bond en avant
startle effrayer
startling ahurissant
starve mourir de faim
stay rester
steadily fixement, fermement
steal (stole stolen) voler, dérober / faire un geste furtif
steal a glance glisser un regard
steal over effleurer
steed cheval de selle
steel acier
step marcher, aller / mesure / seuil
step (take a) faire un pas
stick (get hold of the wrong end of the) comprendre de travers
stiffly plaqué, raide
stifling étouffant
still calme, tranquille, immobile / encore, toujours / néanmoins, quand même
stir troubler, déranger
stone pierre
story histoire, conte
straight honnête, régulier / tout droit
strangely curieusement
strawberry fraise
stream flot / ruisseau
street (up your) dans vos cordes
strength force
stress accent
stretch (s')étendre
strike (struck struck) frapper
string ficelle / rang
string (strung strung) attacher
stroke caresser
strong fort, puissant, solide
strophanthin strophantine, ouabaïne
stud écurie (de course par ex.)
study bureau
stumbling run trot hésitant
stunning fantastique
stunt coup monté, truc
subject soumettre
such tel, tellement, si, tant
such as tel que
suitable adéquat, approprié
sundry (all and) tous, tout le monde
sunlight clarté, soleil
suppress réprimer
sure (to be) c'est certain
sure enough c'est sûr
surge (up) surgir
suspense incertitude
suspicious (be) soupçonner, suspecter
swain soupirant, bon ami
swear (swore sworn) jurer
sweep (swept swept) balayer (du regard)
sweet chéri, amour / parfumé
sweetheart mon cœur, mon ange

sweetly aisément, gentiment
swell chic et riche
swerve virer brusquement
swift rapide
swindler escroc
swine salaud
swing (swung swung) se balancer
syringe seringue

T

taint souiller, polluer
take (took taken) recevoir, accepter
take aback choquer
take away emporter
take back ramener
take off enlever, arracher
take out sortir, emmener
take out of extraire de
talk parler
tall grand
tangled touffu, dense
task travail, tâche
taste goût, intérêt / goûter
tawdry sordide
tearful larmoyant
tell (told told) dire, raconter; compter, avoir de l'importance
tend avoir tendance, être enclin à
term durée, période / rapport, relation
thankful reconnaissant
that is that c'est tout
the one ... the other l'un ... l'autre
theatrical théâtral
then alors, enfin
there voilà
thief voleur
thin mince
thingummybob machin, truc
think (thought thought) penser, supposer
thoroughfare rue, artère
those ces (sg that)
though bien que, cependant
thought pensée
thoughtfully pensivement
thousand mille
thread fil
threat menace
threaten menacer
thrill ravir, transporter de joie
throb palpiter
through à travers / par, à cause de
throughout durant tout
throw (threw thrown) jeter, lancer
throw back rejeter en arrière
thrust (thrust thrust) pousser, fourrer
thus ainsi
tie lien
till jusqu'à ce que
tilt back rabattre
time temps / heure / synchroniser
time (at the) à ce moment-là
timorously timidement
tire fatiguer
tired out épuisé, éreinté
together ensemble
tomorrow demain
too aussi, en plus
too + adj trop
too much trop
tooth (pl teeth) dent
toothbrush brosse à dents
top sommet, bord supérieur
toss lancer, jeter
toss (one's head) secouer (la tête)
touch contact, toucher
towards (en)vers, en direction de
tract terrain, lotissement
train entraîner, dresser
trap piège
tremor tremblement
trite banal, ordinaire
trouble ennuis, problème

true réel, vrai, juste
trump card atout
trust avoir confiance en
truth vérité
try essayer
try it on sb jouer de la patience de qq
turn out éjecter, mettre à la porte
turn to se tourner vers
turn up arriver
turning a hair (without) sans broncher
twist tordre, déformer
twisted smile rictus

U

ubiquitous omniprésent
ugliness laideur
ugly laid, horrible
unbecoming peu flatteur
unbroken continu
uncomfortable mal à l'aise
unconvincingly sans conviction
under sous, au-dessous de
under one's nose sous le nez
undergo subir
underling sous-fifre
undernote trace, touche
understand (understood understood) comprendre
uneasily mal à l'aise
unfair injuste
unfasten détacher
unheeded abandonné
unhindered librement, sans entrave
unless à moins que
unlike différent
unmercifully sans merci
unpleasantness expérience désagréable
unprepossessing déplaisant
unrefreshed fatigué
unsafe dangereux
unscrupulous sans scrupule
untasted pas goûté, pas entamé
unwillingly involontairement
unyielding inflexible
up to jusqu'à
up to (it's) cela dépend de
up to you c'est à vous de
upright droit
upset bouleverser, troubler
upturn renverser
urge pousser (à), presser (de)
use se servir de, utiliser
used habitué
useless inutile
utter absolu, complet

V

van camionnette
velvety soft velouté
view avis, opinion
view (with a ... to) en vue de
vogue popularité
volition volonté

W

wait (for sb) attendre (qq)
waiter garçon, serveur
waitress serveuse
wake (up) (woke woken) se réveiller
walk marcher
wander errer, marcher sans but
wanly faiblement
want vouloir, avoir besoin de
warm enthousiaste
warm-hearted chaleureux
warmth chaleur
warn prévenir
watch regarder, observer
watch montre (bracelet)
watchfulness attention, observation
wave faire un signe de la main ; vague
way façon, moyen
way (by the) en passant

weakly faiblement
wealth richesse
wear (wore worn) porter, avoir sur soi (vêtements…)
weary fatigué, las
weather-beaten buriné
wedding mariage (cérémonie de)
well alors / eh bien
well-bred bien élevé
well done beau travail, bravo
well-known (bien) connu
what ce que, ce qui
what about…? que pensez-vous de… ?
what for pourquoi
whatever quel que soit, tout ce que
whatever happens quoi qu'il arrive
wheel volant (voiture), roue
whenever quand, chaque fois que
where où
which (of) duquel, de laquelle
while moment / tandis que, pendant que
whine se plaindre, gémir
whisper murmure, rumeur / murmurer
whistle sifflement
whiten pâlir
whitewash blanchir à la chaux
whole tout entier
why eh bien / pourquoi
wicked méchant, mauvais
wicker osier
wide grand, agrandi
widen dilater
wife épouse
wild oats erreurs de jeunesse
willingly volontairement
window fenêtre, vitre
wish souhait, désir / vouloir, désirer
wisp fine mèche
wistful nostalgique, pensif
witch sorcière
withdraw (withdrew withdrawn) se retirer
witness témoin
wits (get one's) reprendre ses esprits
woeful malheureux
wonder étonnement ; se demander
wonder (a nine days') un événement
wonderful merveilleux
wont habitué
woo faire la cour à
wood bois, forêt
work travailler
worked up (feel) être dans tous ses états
world monde, univers
worry se faire du souci, s'inquiéter
worse pire
worst (the) (le) pire
worth (be) valoir
worth (your money) pour votre argent
worthy digne, méritant
wrap écharpe, étole
wrathfully avec colère
wrench tirer de toutes ses forces sur
wriggle se tortiller
wrong (le) mal, mauvais, erroné ; qui ne va pas

Y

years ago il y a des années
yet (not) pas encore / cependant / encore, seulement
yield céder

PAPIER À BASE DE FIBRES CERTIFIÉES

Le Livre de Poche s'engage pour l'environnement en réduisant l'empreinte carbone de ses livres. Celle de cet exemplaire est de :
200 g éq. CO_2
Rendez-vous sur www.livredepoche-durable.fr

Achevé d'imprimer en décembre 2016 en Espagne par
CPI
Dépôt légal 1re publication : novembre 2006
Édition 09 – décembre 2016
LIBRAIRIE GÉNÉRALE FRANÇAISE – 21, rue du Montparnasse – 75298 Paris Cedex 06

30/8409/2